QUICK & EASY

MEXICAN COOKING

QUICK & EASY

MEXICAN COOKING

More than 80 Everyday Recipes

BY CECILIA HAE-JIN LEE

PHOTOGRAPHS BY LEIGH BEISCH

CHRONICLE BOOKS
SAN FRANCISCO

Library of Congress Cataloging-in-Publication Data available.
ISBN: 978-0-8118-7232-4

Manufactured in China

Designed by Andrew Schapiro
Prop styling by Philippine Scali
Food styling by Robyn Valarik
Typesetting by DC Typography, Inc.

10 9 8 7 6 5 4 3 2

Chronicle Books LLC
680 Second Street
San Francisco, California 94107
www.chroniclebooks.com

TABLE OF CONTENTS

❧ INTRODUCTION ❧

Living in Los Angeles, I was introduced to Mexican cuisine at a young age. I don't know if the first dish I tried was the beef enchiladas smothered in red sauce and cheese from the school cafeteria or the spicy burritos I got from the taco truck down the street. Growing up, I had my share of fake nachos and imposter tacos in hard shells that came from shrink-wrapped boxes, but I also had my fill of home-made tamales and steaming bowls of *menudo*.

However, my real education in Mexican cuisine began when my parents bought a Mexican grocery store in the San Fernando Valley.

It was the summer before I started high school, the early '80s, and the height of Valley Girl culture. After school, our friends would find my siblings and me, still in our Catholic-school uniforms, running the cash register, taking inventory, and stacking boxes and boxes of tomatoes. The *banda* music would be blaring from the radio while we worked beneath a canopy of colorful piñatas, their tissue-paper fringe flapping in the breeze of the swamp cooler.

I learned how to pick the perfect avocado, how to wrap corn husks to make giant stacks of tamales, and how to clean the spikes off *nopalitos* without pricking my fingers.

I experimented with varieties of peppers, made my way through bowls of salsa, and devoured papayas doused with lime juice and chili powder.

Our customers and friends would bring us culinary wonders from their kitchens—bowls brimming with pork meatballs, moist cakes sprinkled with cinnamon, and handmade tortillas still warm from their stoves. From these *abuelas* (grandmas) and *tías* (aunts), I learned secrets of each family's mole, where to get the best chocolates, and how to turn out rows and rows of enchiladas without even breaking a sweat.

I took these lessons with me to college, perfecting my soups, making my salsas spicier, and learning more of the street Spanish I have yet to master. After graduation,

I lived in Mexico and tasted the real flavors south of the border. Strangers would invite me into their kitchens where we would cook, sing, and laugh together.

The origins of Mexican food go back centuries to the culture of the Aztec, the Maya, the Toltec, and the Olmec. The nomadic Maya began to farm the land. They ate corn tortillas, made bean paste, hunted wild game, fished from the ocean, and enjoyed the tropical fruits of the region. The Aztec added to this already developed pantry the fire of chile peppers and the wonderful flavors from cacao. Then throw in the culinary influence of the Spanish, who brought wheat, domesticated animals, grain mills, and cheesemaking. With more visitors and traders to Mexico, the cuisines of France, Portugal, West Africa, the Caribbean, and South America were added to the mix, and we have the modern Mexican menu that is alive and kicking today.

A wonderful example of the richness of Mexican entrees is *mole*, which is a term used for a variety of thick sauces that vary in color and flavor depending on the ingredients. Each region has its own variation. Oaxaca, the heart of Mexico in both geography and food, has several different varieties. One of the most popular kinds, *mole poblano*, is an excellent example of how history and contact with various cultures were necessary to shape the dish. A bowl of mole poblano might contain peanuts, sesame seeds, anise, cinnamon, black pepper, sugar, salt, garlic, onion, cloves, coriander, tomato, raisins, lard, and chocolate. The individual ingredients made their way to Mexico at different times, but all of them together create a complex and delicious dish that could have only originated in Mexico.

Even American food has infiltrated the kitchens south of the border with the invention of Tex-Mex cuisine. Although the marriage of American fare and Mexican delicacies probably happened centuries ago, the term

"Tex-Mex" started as a reference to the Texas-Mexican railway around 1875. The term wasn't used to describe food until the latter half of the twentieth century. Items such as chili con carne, fajitas, and tortilla chips all emerged from this culinary marriage and what we know as Mexican food in America has been largely shaped by this history.

Traditional Mexican food was cooked over an open fire on iron skillets (called *comals*) or in ceramic pots. There was no oven cooking, per se, but food was fried, steamed, or boiled. From this way of cooking emerged long-stewed meats boiled into soups, shredded into fillings flavored with chile pastes and nuts, and wrapped up in a blanket of tortillas. Seafood from the coastal lands added more flavors to the diet.

Today, we get to enjoy centuries of food traditions with minimal effort. Mexican food is so popular that ingredients are readily available almost anywhere. Although there is a time and a place for spending long hours slaving over a hot stove, I believe that we can enjoy the best of the feast without too much labor.

I've simplified the recipes that I've carried along from my youth, picked up along the way, and researched from my travels. I can still get a weeknight dinner on the table without compromising the delicious flavors and complex aromas that make Mexican food one of my favorite cuisines of all time.

I wrote this book hoping I could inspire home cooks to get out and bury their noses in fragrant bouquets of fresh cilantro, experiment with wonderfully fiery chiles, and explore the regional flavors of Mexico for themselves. So, get out the *metate* (mortar), cradle the ripe tomatoes in your hands, and get ready to start the culinary journey of a lifetime.

❧ PANTRY NOTES ❧

The Mexican pantry is filled with fragrant herbs, fresh vegetables, and dried chiles. The good news is that you probably have many of the necessary ingredients in your pantry already, but feel free to check the glossary (page 15) if any of them are unfamiliar to you.

I've divided the ingredients list into three sections. The A-list includes those used most often and found in a Mexican kitchen. The B-list has items that you should have around if you want to make Mexican food often.

The C-list ingredients are those used for special dishes and worth having if you're an adventurous cook and want to expand your Mexican food repertoire.

Luckily, it's easy these days to find the ingredients you'll need to make delicious Mexican food at home. Even your non-Latino supermarket will likely have many of the items you need to get started. So, roll up your sleeves and get ready for your Mexican food adventure. Let's get cooking!

A-LIST
INGREDIENTS

BEANS
CHEESES
(see "Guide to Mexican Cheeses," page 20)
CILANTRO
CINNAMON
CORN
CUMIN
GARLIC
JALAPEÑO PEPPERS
LIMES
ONIONS
RICE
SERRANO CHILES
TOMATOES
TORTILLAS
VANILLA

B-LIST
INGREDIENTS

ANCHO CHILES
CANNED CHIPOTLE PEPPERS
CHILI POWDER
CREMA
MASA
NOPALES
PLANTAINS
POBLANO or PASILLA CHILES
TOMATILLOS

C-LIST
INGREDIENTS

ANNATTO SEEDS
CHAYOTE
EPAZOTE
HOMINY
JAMAICA
JÍCAMA
PILONCILLO
PRICKLY PEARS
TAMARIND PODS

Glossary of Mexican
⌁ INGREDIENTS ⌁

ANCHO CHILE: The dried version of either poblano or pasilla chiles, this milder chile is often ground and made into powder for flavoring recipes.

ANNATTO (ACHIOTE) SEEDS: Annatto are the seeds and the surrounding red pulp of the achiote plant. They're sometimes used to make red food dye and are used in Mexican cuisine as a spice. They're slightly sweet, peppery, and earthy in flavor, with a hint of nutmeg. Achiote is sold both whole and ground, but I prefer to buy it whole and grind it myself to get the best flavor. The seeds add a wonderful flavor and color to meats, rice, and tamales.

CHAYOTE: In the same family as zucchini, cucumbers, and melons, chayote is a staple in Mexican cuisine. They are shaped like flat avocados, but are hard, light green vegetables with lumpy, wrinkled outsides. They can be eaten raw, baked, fried, broiled, mashed, pickled, or however you want. They are a little slimy when cut, with a largish pit inside. Everything on this plant (even the root, stems, leaves, and seed) is edible. Chayotes have a mild flavor and are high in vitamin C.

CHEESE (QUESO): There are several types of cheeses available in Mexican markets. I've included a "Guide to Mexican Cheeses" (page 20) to help you navigate the different varieties you may run into.

CHIPOTLE: Chipotles are smoky, deep-red chile peppers made by roasting ripe jalapeños. The Aztecs invented a way of smoking the chiles first before drying them, since the fleshy jalapeños were prone to rot instead of drying properly. Similar to smoking meats, this method of drying allows the chiles to be preserved while maintaining most of their flavor. A medium-spicy pepper, chipotles can be found whole dried, powdered, pickled, or canned in adobo sauce. I prefer to use the canned versions for their complex flavor.

CILANTRO (CORIANDER): Although all parts of the coriander plant are edible, we find its green leaves used the most in Mexican cuisine (and the word *cilantro*, derived from Spanish, refers to the leaves). Cilantro is a popular ingredient for salsas and guacamole, but the leaves can be chopped and added to tacos or sprinkled on as a garnish, as well.

CINNAMON (CANELA): Mexican cinnamon tastes slightly different and tends to be a little softer and looser than the bark grown in other countries. Cinnamon bark can be easily ground in a spice grinder or a *molcajete*, a traditional stone mortar and pestle, usually made from basalt.

CREMA: The Mexican version of crème fraîche, prepared versions of crema are readily available in the refrigerated dairy section or fresh delis of Latino groceries. However, you can make your own version pretty easily. Combine equal parts sour cream and whipping cream and blend together until smooth. Squeeze in some lime juice if you like your crema with a citrus note.

CUMIN (CUMINO): Unlike chile peppers, which made their way east from the Americas, cumin is an Arabic spice (native to Syria) that was imported by the Spanish to the Americas. A member of the parsley family, the cumin plant's seeds are sold whole or ground. I like to have both types available for different dishes.

EPAZOTE: This is an herb that grows wild in Mexico and parts of the southwestern United States. Sometimes called pigweed or wormseed in English, it's used mainly as an ingredient when cooking black beans to help ward off gastric disturbances later. Older leaves can be quite bitter, whereas younger leaves are milder in flavor. Use sparingly since it is said to be poisonous in large quantities.

HOMINY (NIXTAMAL): Hominy is made from dried corn kernels (maize) that have been treated with lime (calcium hydroxide) or another alkali solution, then soaked in water to soften them. The kernels are used in soups like menudo or pozole. When it's ground into a fine powder it becomes masa flour, used to make tortillas and tamales. You can find both yellow and white hominy in cans at most grocery stores.

JAMAICA (HIBISCUS): Pronounced "huh-MY-kuh," jamaica (dried hibiscus petals) is sold in Latin markets (sometimes labeled "flor de Jamaica") to be used to make the vibrantly red drink Hibiscus Punch (page 153).

JÍCAMA: Jícama is a crispy root vegetable native to Latin America. A relative of the bean family, it can be found year-round in Mexican and Central American markets. Look for jícamas that are relatively heavy for their size, since they should be juicy and not dry. They should have unblemished skins and dry roots. Store them unpeeled in your crisper drawer for up to three weeks.

LIME (LIMA or LIMÓN VERDE): In Mexico, they don't often distinguish between limes and lemons, calling them both *limón*, unless they want to be specific, and then they add the *verde* (green) to specify lime. That might be because limes are more readily available than lemons and are used in cooking, made into fresh beverages, or just sliced and served on the side of carne asada, fish tacos, or any number of recipes. The most common variety found in the country is what we know as Key limes in America. Although you can substitute the larger, darker, Persian limes, use Key limes if you want to be more authentic.

MANGO: Mexican mangoes are larger than their Indian or Southeast Asian cousins and are used to make aguas frescas, paletas, puddings, and more. You can find street vendors in Mexico selling fresh mangoes sprinkled with lime, chili powder, and a bit of salt for a tangy, sweet, salty, spicy treat.

MASA: Used to make tortillas, empanadas, or tamales, this is a special type of corn flour, made from hominy. Look for masa that only contains corn and calcium hydroxide as ingredients. It's sometimes called masa harina (*harina* means flour).

NOPALE: Also called "nopalitos," nopales are the flat, paddle-like prickly pear leaves that grow wild in the deserts of Mexico and the southwestern United States. Technically, "nopal" means cactus in Spanish; "nopales" are the cactus stems; and "nopalitos" refers to the paddles once they are cut off and prepared for eating. To remove the thorns, hold the end of the cactus with a pair of tongs and cut off the thorns in a flicking motion with a paring knife, similar to sharpening a pencil with a razor blade. Lucky for you, they are sold fresh with their thorns removed in most Mexican markets. Some even sell them already cut into strips. If you can't find them fresh where you live, they are also available in jars.

PASILLA CHILE: Sometimes called "chiles negro," these are the dark green versions of poblano chiles. These chiles have shiny skins and pointy tips and vary from mild to medium spicy. In Oaxaca, they smoke and dry these flavorful peppers to spice up their mole negro.

PILONCILLO (BROWN SUGAR): Mexican brown sugar gets its name from its traditional cone shape. The dark variety, which is called *oscuro*, is heavy in molasses, and is more common. The lighter *blanco* is also available. Piloncillo is used to make a variety of hot drinks and candies. You can buy the cones in varying sizes, usually in the spice or produce aisle of Mexican groceries. Substitute dark brown sugar if you don't have a Latino market nearby.

PLANTAIN (PLÁTANO): These large relatives of the banana can't be eaten raw, but are positively mouthwatering when cooked and topped with sugar. They have hard skins that go from green to yellow to black when completely ripened. For sweet dishes, you'll want to use the ones that are nearly black.

POBLANO CHILE: Available in most Latin American markets, poblanos are a mild green pepper originating from Puebla. The darker varieties are called pasillas, and called anchos or mulatos when dried. They're most commonly used in making chiles rellenos and chiles en nogada.

PRICKLY PEAR (TUNA): See also Nopales. Prickly pear is the English name of the cactus from which we get both nopales (the plant "paddles") and the fruit (called "tuna" in Spanish).

TAMARIND (TAMARINDO): Originating from the tropical forests of Africa, tamarind migrated to India and parts of Southeast Asia. It was introduced to Mexico and parts of South America by Portuguese explorers in the sixteenth century. The pods are ripe when they become a brown (or reddish brown) color and they can be opened easily with bare fingers. Both sweet and tangy, tamarindo is used to make candies and aguas frescas in Mexico. The pods are available in the produce sections of Mexican, Indian, and Southeast Asian markets. You'll know the pods are fresh if the outer shell separates from the fruit pulp when you bend it in half. Older pods can be reconstituted by soaking in hot water. They'll keep in a zipper bag in the refrigerator or freezer for a few weeks, but they're best used fresh.

TOMATILLO: It's no surprise that this Aztec fruit is related to the tomato. Their name translates to "little tomato." They look like smaller, green versions of their red cousins, but are much more tart. They grow inside paper-thin husks that open to let you know that the fruits are ready to harvest. You'll find them fresh, many with their husks still on, and canned in Latino and regular markets. When buying them fresh, look for firm, bright green fruits (they get yellower when they ripen too much). Fresh tomatillos will keep for two to three weeks in the coldest part of the refrigerator. They can also be sliced and frozen in airtight bags, although they'll lose a bit of their distinct tart flavor.

VANILLA: Vanilla is the fruit of a thick orchid vine that grows wild along the edges of Mexico's tropical rain forests. The Aztecs fermented and dried the beans to develop vanillin, a white crystalline substance that "grew" on the outside of the dark bean that they added to their *xocolatl* drinks. Although most of the commercially available vanilla beans today come from Madagascar, Mexican vanilla beans are thicker and darker and are considered the best in flavor and quality.

Guide to Mexican
➤ CHEESES ➤

Although the size of markets in Mexico ranges from tiny village tianguis *to sprawling urban affairs that span several blocks, they all have wonderful arrangements of* quesos— *rolled in twine, twisted up like string, wrapped in corn husks, or coated with red spices.*

Since the Spaniards introduced cows and goats to the New World, Mexicans have developed their own regional special- ties and different ways of making cheese. I'm including this little note to help you make some sense of the varieties you'll find in your favorite Latin American market.

Fresh Cheeses

PANELA: Adapted from the Greek "basket cheese," it is soft, white, and absorbs flavors so well that it's sometimes sold coated with a garlic paste or wrapped in toasted avocado leaves. Because of the imprint of the basket in which it's often molded, it is also called "queso de canasta."

QUESO BLANCO: Made from skimmed milk, this creamy white cheese is very mild in flavor. Traditionally cured with lemon juice, it's now commercially made with the less fragrant rennet. It's like mozzarella, but less stringy, and it's white (hence the name). It gets soft when heated, but doesn't melt, so it's a good choice for stuffing enchiladas. You can use mozzarella as a substitute.

QUESO FRESCO: Its name translating to "fresh cheese," this white cheese crumbles when broken, since it's made from a combination of cow's and goat's milks. It is often used in taquitos and chiles rellenos or used to top *botanas* (appetizers). Monterey Jack makes a good substitute.

REQUESÓN: This cheese looks like ricotta, but it tastes mild, not salty. Although not widely available outside of Mexico, if you can find it, you'll see it wrapped in fresh corn husks. It's often used as a filling in rellenos, sopes, enchiladas or in desserts. A mild ricotta can be substituted.

Oaxaca

Asadero

Queso Blanco

Crema

Oaxaca

Cotija

Soft and Semisoft Cheeses

AÑEJO: Although it's considered a soft cheese, this aged version of queso fresco can become quite firm and salty. It's usually crumbled or grated over food to serve as a garnish or to add a bit of extra flavor. You can substitute a mild romano cheese in its place.

ASADERO: A cheese specifically for melting, asadero is used for *fundido*, Mexico's version of fondue. Monterey Jack or fontina cheeses make a fine substitute.

QUESO CHIHUAHUA: You can tell this cheese from most other Mexican cheeses because of its pale yellow color. It varies from mild to sharp, depending on where it's made. A medium Cheddar or sharper Jack cheeses make a fine substitute.

QUESO JALAPEÑO: This soft white cheese with bits of jalapeños in it makes a good addition to spicy quesadillas.

QUESO OAXACA: This stretched, slightly tangy curd cheese is kneaded and wound into balls. The most popular cheese for making quesadillas, it's also called "quesillo." You can substitute mozzarella or string cheese.

Firm and Semifirm Cheeses

QUESO AÑEJO ENCHILADO: The name translates to "aged cheese in chile," and that's what it is. The cheese is coated with a red chile or paprika and then aged to give it a firmer texture and stronger flavor. It is good to include in a cheese platter or to serve with crackers.

QUESO COTIJA: Named after the town in Mochocaca where it was created, this is a crumbly goat cheese that is usually served over beans and salads.

QUESO CRIOLLO: One of the few pale yellow cheeses from Mexico, it's usually produced around the Taxco and Guerrero areas. A gratable cheese, it's very similar to Muenster.

QUESO MANCHEGO: Imported from the La Mancha region of Spain, this buttery, yellow cheese is good for melting or serving with fruit and crackers.

QUESO MANCHEGO VIEJO: As the name suggests, this is manchego cheese that has been aged to make it harder and sharper in flavor. It's usually served grated over appetizer dishes.

⋟ UTENSILS ⋞

for Cooking Mexican Food

BAKING PAN: You want to have a deep, rectangular baking pan for making enchiladas, tres leches cake, and other things. I prefer glass pans because you can see the food as it cooks, and they're easier to clean, but metal pans work just as fine.

COMAL OR CAST-IRON SKILLET: Great for cooking tortillas, whipping up some quesadillas, or making sizzling fresh fajitas.

DUTCH OVEN OR HEAVY-BOTTOMED LARGE POT: You'll want a large pot that distributes heat evenly for boiling meats, making beans, or even for deep-frying (the high sides help keep the oil from splattering). It's also good for making big cauldrons of soup on those cold winter nights.

FOOD PROCESSOR OR BLENDER: Although these appliances weren't available until the recent few decades, there's no reason to forgo modern conveniences just to be traditional. A food processor or blender is a must for making aguas frescas, blended margaritas, creamy soups, and all those varieties of salsas you'll want to try.

GLOVES: Plastic or food-safe gloves are the best if you want to save your skin from the unforgiving oil of cut chiles. Although the chiles don't burn the skin on my hands, I've found myself crying sad tears, accidentally having rubbed my eyes after chopping up a bunch of serranos.

LIME PRESS: When you get in the habit of cooking Mexican food, you'll find that a lime press will be one of your best friends in the kitchen. Not only does it save your hands from having to squeeze dozens of limes, but it catches the seeds so you don't have to waste your time picking them out of your salsas.

MOLCAJETE: An old-fashioned mortar and pestle, this stone tool dates back to a time even before the Aztec and Maya cultures. Every Mexican family has one of these in its kitchen. They're used to crush spices, make salsas, or mash avocados. The rough surface of the basalt stone makes for good grinding with the *tejolote* (the grinding tool). A wonderful instrument, the molcajete also works well as a serving dish to make your salsas look even more authentic. Look for the dark, black basalt stone and don't fall for the imitation gray ones made of concrete.

ROLLING PIN: If you don't have a tortilla press, you can roll your own with a rolling pin (see page 44).

SPICE GRINDER: This handy gadget is great for getting the freshest flavors from spices and for grinding your own chili powder. If you don't have one, you can use a clean coffee grinder to get the same effect.

TORTILLA PRESS: Although not necessary for making your own tortillas, this handy kitchen gadget does make it easier for you to crank out homemade tortillas. Inexpensive (usually costing $15 to $20), they're made of wood, cast iron, or aluminum and can be found in Mexican markets or even general discount stores.

1

SALSAS, TORTILLAS, AND MORE

(Salsas, Tortillas y Mas)

Salsas are the heart and soul of Mexican cooking. Can you imagine a hot pile of tortilla chips, fresh from the fryer, with nothing to dip them in? And think of how naked the tray of enchiladas would be without a fine coat of red or green sauce to cover them.

The Mexican salsa has at its heart the chile pepper. The variety and number of chiles found in this great land is fantastic. There are jalapeños, serranos, habaneros, poblanos, pasillas, piquíns, moritas, mulatos, cascabels, guajillos, and so on and so forth. These chiles are ground in a molcajete with other ingredients to make the colorful varieties of sauces found in Mexican cuisine.

There is an endless variety of sauces that can be made from spicy peppers, red ripe tomatoes, fine green toma-tillos, or the wonderful aromatic combination of spices that makes up the moles that grace our tables. Every region, each town, and all families have such wonderful varieties of their own that I could fill a whole book on just the joyful salsa combinations. But since I want to share other flavors and recipes with you, I've overstuffed this chapter with some basics like the Chunky Avocado Dip (page 36) or Roasted Tomatillo Salsa (page 33)—dips and salsas you can whip up for a weeknight dinner or double or triple to amp up any celebration.

The most basic of Mexican salsas includes tomatoes, onions, garlic, chiles, cilantro, and a bit of lime, as in the "Rooster's Beak" Salsa (page 31). Inspired by the tempting piles of ripe tomatoes at my folks' market, I've made end-less varieties of this as an after-school snack.

I've also included more unusual sauces, like the Herbed Pumpkin Seed Mole (page 41), that can add excitement to any kind of meat or fish or can be poured over a plate of cheese enchiladas. The Achiote Paste (page 39) can be rubbed on pork, fish, chicken, or even tofu to dress them up with a fiery red coating.

This chapter is a primer to help you get started in the cooking of Mexican dishes. The great thing about sauces is that they are very forgiving. So feel free to add your own flair and adjust things to your own tastes. Add an extra serrano pepper or two to kick up the heat a bit, or tone down the fire if you have a delicate palate. Adjust with your favorite ingredient, try something unusual, and make your own family favorite. Double or triple a recipe to share jars with friends and neighbors.

Then, warm up some tortillas or cook up some tortilla chips, kick back, and enjoy.

Here's a handy little chart with heat-indicating Scoville Units (developed by chemist Wilbur Scoville in 1912), so that you can choose your peppers wisely:

Pepper Varieties	Heat Rating	Scoville Unit Range
Sweet bell, sweet banana, pimiento	0	0 (negligible)
Cherry, New Mexico, pepperoncini, Sonora	1	100–1,000
Anaheim, ancho, pasilla, Española, New Mexico, mulato	2	1,000–1,500
Cascabel, Sandia	3	1,500–2,500
Jalapeño, poblano, chipotle, mirasol, guajillo	4	2,500–5,000
Serrano, hot wax, Hidalgo, manzano	5	5,000–15,000
Chile de arbol	6	15,000–30,000
Cayenne, pequín, aji, Tabasco	7	30,000–50,000
Thai, chiltepín, santaka, yatsafusa	8	50,000–100,000
Orange habanero, Scotch bonnet, Jamaican hot, Caribbean red	9	100,000–350,000
Red savina habanero, chocolate habanero, Indian Tezpur	10	350,000 and up

➤ "ROOSTER'S BEAK" SALSA ➤
(Pico de Gallo)

Pico de gallo translates to "beak of the rooster." Perhaps it's called this because of the ruby red tomatoes looking akin to the color of a rooster's beak. Or maybe because all of the ingredients are chopped together like chicken feed. Whatever the origin of the name, it's used to describe any number of salsas in Mexican cuisine. My version is derived from the most popular kind made with tomatoes, onion, cilantro, and chiles. Feel free to personalize it to fit your taste buds. Serve with a side of tortilla chips.

MAKES 4 CUPS

2 pounds Roma or vine-ripened tomatoes
½ medium onion
1 packed cup coarsely chopped fresh cilantro, stems cut
1 jalapeño pepper
2 garlic cloves
2 limes
1 teaspoon ground cumin
1 teaspoon freshly ground black pepper
1 teaspoon salt

Chop the tomatoes into small cubes and put them into a large bowl.

In a food processor, pulse the onion until it is finely chopped (be careful not to overprocess or it'll get mushy). Scrape it into the bowl with the tomatoes.

In the same processor, add the cilantro and pulse until chopped. Add to the bowl with the tomato and onion.

Cut the jalapeño in half, lengthwise, discarding the stem (discard the seeds and veins if you think it'll be too spicy). Pulse the jalapeño and garlic in the processor until finely minced. Scrape into the bowl with the other vegetables.

Cut the limes in half and squeeze their juices into the tomato mixture. Add the cumin, black pepper, and salt, adding a bit more salt to your taste. Toss together before serving.

NOTE: *Double the recipe for a large party or if you want to have some left over for later meals. You can serve it immediately, but it'll taste better if you let it sit for a bit so the flavors can commingle.*

➤ SMOKY CHIPOTLE SALSA ➤

(Salsa con Chipotle)

Chipotle chile peppers are smoked jalapeños. They look very different from the green peppers you know and love because the jalapeños are red and ripe before being turned into delicious chipotle peppers. You can find them dried or canned in adobo sauce. These peppers are characterized as "medium" in heat, but when you use as many as I do in this recipe, they can get a bit spicy. Serve this salsa with a side of chips or over grilled meats.

MAKES ABOUT 5 CUPS

2 tablespoons olive oil

12 garlic cloves, sliced

1 onion, chopped

3 cups chipotle peppers in adobo sauce

8 Roma tomatoes, coarsely chopped

2 tablespoons salt

2 tablespoons freshly squeezed lime juice

½ teaspoon freshly ground black pepper

Heat the olive oil in a large skillet over high heat. Add the garlic and onion and let them brown, stirring only a couple of times (about 2 minutes). Add the chipotle with adobo sauce and the tomatoes and cook for an additional 3 to 4 minutes until heated through.

Carefully pour the mixture into a blender or food processor. Add the salt, lime juice, and black pepper and blend until smooth.

Serve immediately or save it in the refrigerator for a few days.

VARIATION: *If you're having a hard time finding the canned peppers, you can substitute about 30 dried chipotle peppers, rehydrated and minced.*

❧ ROASTED TOMATILLO SALSA ❧

(Salsa Verde)

Salsa verde is usually a tangier, milder salsa than the more popular tomato-based salsas. Fresh tomatillos can be found in Latino markets. They look like tiny green tomatoes, but grow inside thin skins. Although boiling the tomatillos is common, roasting brings out more flavor. Refrigerate any leftovers and the salsa will be even better the next day. Serve with a side of tortilla chips, on top of freshly cooked fish, over Stuffed Peppers (page 91), or as a condiment to accompany any of your dishes.

MAKES 3 CUPS

1½ pounds (12 to 15) tomatillos, husked and washed

1   small (or ½ medium) onion, quartered

4 or 5 garlic cloves

1   bunch fresh cilantro, stems cut

1   jalapeño, stemmed and halved

1   teaspoon salt

Preheat the broiler.

Cut the tomatillos in half and place them, cut-sides down, on a foil-lined baking sheet. Place under a broiler until the skins are somewhat blackened on top, 8 to 10 minutes.

Carefully pierce the tomatillos with a fork and put them in a food processor or blender. Add the onion and garlic and process until combined. Add the cilantro, jalapeño, and salt and process until puréed.

Go ahead; taste it before serving and add a bit more salt, if you think it needs it.

NOTE: *Depending on the ripeness of your tomatillos, the salsa might be a bit tangier than you like. (You can see that this recipe doesn't require any limes.) If you find it so, feel free to add ¼ to ½ teaspoon of sugar to make the salsa just right for your palate.*

⇜ MANGO SALSA ⇝

(Salsa de Mango)

This is a refreshing salsa during hot weather. Use mangoes that are ripe, but not soft. The skins should be mostly red and yellow and the fruit should be fragrant when you hold it up to your nose. This salsa works especially well served with meaty fish (like swordfish, mahi mahi, or salmon) that has been grilled on a summer's night, or with a side of chips.

MAKES ABOUT 3½ CUPS

1 ripe mango (peel and pit discarded), diced (about 1½ cups)

2 or 3 ripe tomatoes, diced (about 1½ cups)

½ medium red onion, finely chopped

½ cup or more coarsely chopped fresh cilantro

2 tablespoons freshly squeezed lime juice

1 serrano pepper, minced

2 garlic cloves, minced

½ teaspoon salt

½ teaspoon freshly ground black pepper

In a medium bowl, combine the mango, tomatoes, onion, cilantro, lime juice, serrano, and garlic. Add the salt and black pepper and toss. Let sit for about 5 minutes, then taste to see if you need to add a bit more salt or black pepper to your liking.

Cover and refrigerate for about 30 minutes or serve immediately.

NOTE: *Discard the seeds and veins of the pepper if you don't want your salsa to be too spicy.*

CHUNKY
≈ AVOCADO DIP ≈
(Guacamole)

This is a little more elaborate than your basic guacamole, but it's still not difficult to make. Feel free to double or quadruple the recipe for a generous party-size portion. I prefer to use the Hass avocados (the kind with the black skin), but any variety will do. Serve with a side of tortilla chips.

MAKES 2 CUPS

- 2 ripe avocados
- 1 ripe tomato, chopped
- ½ cup coarsely chopped fresh cilantro, plus extra for garnish
- ⅓ cup finely chopped onion
- 2 tablespoons freshly squeezed lime juice
- 1 tablespoon olive oil
- 1 garlic clove, minced
-    Salt
-    Freshly ground black pepper

Cut the avocados in half and remove the pits (see page 57). Scoop the avocado flesh into a medium bowl and mash with a fork. Don't worry about mashing all the avocado smooth, since the extra chunks add to the fun texture. Add the tomato, cilantro, onion, lime juice, olive oil, and garlic and mix. Season with salt and black pepper and sprinkle with some additional cilantro, if you wish.

Serve immediately.

NOTE: *If you want an extra kick, add a little bit of chopped jalapeño or serrano pepper (seeds and veins removed, if you want it less spicy). If you need to refrigerate your guacamole, completely cover the surface with plastic wrap so that no air is touching the avocado. There is a myth that putting the pit in keeps the avocado from browning, but it doesn't work—only the part covered by the avocado seed keeps from oxidizing. Not very useful.*

RED ENCHILADA SAUCE

(Salsa Roja)

Although red enchilada sauce is readily available in most grocery stores, I prefer to make my own. It doesn't take that long and the flavor is so much better. You can easily double or triple the batch and freeze any leftovers for subsequent meals.

MAKES 2½ CUPS

- 3 tablespoons vegetable oil
- 1 tablespoon flour
- ¼ cup chili powder
- 2 cups chicken broth
- Two 5-ounce cans tomato sauce
- 3 tablespoons garlic powder
- 1 teaspoon dried or 1 tablespoon chopped fresh oregano
- 1 teaspoon ground cumin
- ½ teaspoon salt
- ¼ teaspoon sugar
- ¼ teaspoon ground cinnamon

Heat the vegetable oil in a medium saucepan over medium heat. Add the flour and stir, smoothing it out to make a roux, and cook for about 1 minute. Add the chili powder and cook for an additional 30 seconds. Add the broth, tomato sauce, garlic powder, oregano, cumin, salt, sugar, and cinnamon and stir to combine.

Increase the heat and bring to a boil, then reduce the heat to medium and cook until the flavors deepen, an additional 15 minutes.

Remove from the heat and use in your favorite enchilada recipe, pour over burritos to make them "wet," or to make tamales. If you're not using the sauce right away, store it in a glass jar with a tightly fitting lid in the refrigerator for up to 1 week.

VARIATION: *To make a vegetarian version, replace the chicken broth with vegetable broth. If you find that this sauce is too spicy for you, reduce the chili powder to your taste.*

ANCHO CHILE SAUCE

(Salsa de Chile de Ancho)

This is a nice and spicy sauce that's also versatile. Pour it over your enchiladas rojo, a nicely grilled fish, or some baked chicken, or just have it with a side of crispy tortilla chips.

MAKES ABOUT 2½ CUPS

2 ancho chiles
1 tablespoon vegetable oil
¼ cup chopped onion
2 cups chicken broth
2 tomatoes, chopped
¼ cup raisins
1 teaspoon dried or 1 tablespoon fresh oregano
½ teaspoon ground cumin

Remove the stems and seeds of the chiles and soak them in hot water for 10 minutes. Remove the chiles and chop them.

In a large saucepan, heat the vegetable oil over high heat. Add the chiles and onion and sauté until tender, about 5 minutes. Add the broth, tomatoes, raisins, oregano, and cumin and bring to a boil. Reduce the heat and let simmer until the tomatoes are cooked, another 10 minutes.

Carefully pour all of the contents into a food processor or blender and process until smooth. Serve immediately, or store in a tightly sealed container in the refrigerator for up to 1 week.

ACHIOTE PASTE

(Recado Colorado)

Although this fiery red seasoning is traditionally used to make *cochinita pibil* (see page 116), a lovely pork dish, it makes a nice rub for chicken, meaty fish, or even thick cuts of vegetables you might throw on the grill. Annatto seeds ground into a paste are particularly popular in Oaxacan and Yucatan dishes. Be sure to wear gloves and use nonreactive utensils because the achiote will stain everything (including your hands) a nice *rojo* (red) color!

MAKES ABOUT ¾ CUP

5 tablespoons achiote (annatto) seeds
1 tablespoon black peppercorns
2 teaspoons cumin seeds
8 whole allspice berries
½ teaspoon whole cloves
½ cup freshly squeezed orange juice
3 habanero peppers, seeded
10 garlic cloves
2 tablespoons salt
½ cup freshly squeezed lemon juice (about 5 lemons)
¼ cup olive oil

In a food processor, pulse-grind the achiote seeds, peppercorns, cumin, allspice, and cloves to a fine powder. Add the orange juice, habaneros, garlic, and salt and blend until smooth. Blend in the lemon juice and olive oil until a paste is formed.

Wrap tablespoon-sized portions of the paste in plastic and store in the freezer for months—although it never lasts that long in our house!

NOTE: *If you don't want your paste to light your mouth on fire, you can substitute jalapeños for the habaneros, or omit the hot peppers altogether for a fragrant, but mild seasoning.*

❧ PUMPKIN SEED MOLE ❧

(Mole Verde con Hierbas)

In Oaxaca, green mole (*mole verde*) is one of the seven famous moles. What makes this one different is not just the lack of chocolate, but also the addition of fresh herbs, which give it a fabulous green color. Of course, every region or family has its own way of making mole. I learned this recipe from my friend from Puebla, who calls it "mole pipían," referring to the pumpkin seeds used in it. Whatever you call it, it's fantastic with chicken, fish, or pork, or as a spicy sauce over a bunch of enchiladas.

MAKES ABOUT 3 CUPS

- 1   cup peeled pumpkin seeds
- 1   teaspoon cumin seeds
- ½   teaspoon dried oregano
- 1   tablespoon vegetable or olive oil
- 1   onion, cut into wedges
- 5   tomatillos, husked and halved
- 5   garlic cloves, halved
- 2   jalapeño peppers, sliced
- 2   cups chicken broth
- 1   packed cup coarsely chopped fresh cilantro
- 1   cup coarsely chopped fresh parsley
- ½   cup fresh epazote (optional)
- 1   teaspoon salt

In a large skillet with high sides or in a large saucepan, toast the pumpkin seeds, cumin seeds, and oregano over high heat. Toss to make sure they don't burn, but toast until fragrant, 3 to 4 minutes. Remove from the heat and transfer to a blender or spice grinder and process until ground. Set aside.

In the same skillet, heat the oil over medium-high heat. Add the onion, tomatillos, garlic, and jalapeños and cook until slightly browned, 4 to 5 minutes, tossing a couple of times, but not stirring too much. Carefully place the vegetables in a blender or food processor. Then add the broth, cilantro, parsley, epazote (if using), and salt and process until puréed. Pour back into the skillet and add the ground pumpkin seed mixture. Let simmer until the flavors are well combined, about 15 minutes, stirring occasionally.

Serve immediately. Any leftovers can be refrigerated in an airtight container for a couple of days.

NOTE: *If you don't have a spice grinder, a clean coffee grinder works great and a blender works fine, too. If you can't find epazote, you can substitute the green tops of radishes or just leave them out altogether.*

⋟ CORN TORTILLAS ⋞
(*Tortillas de Maiz*)

In Mexico, tortillas are usually made fresh every day and served hot off the griddle. Once you taste these, it'll be hard to go back to store-bought again. Masa harina is a special corn flour used to make tortillas. You can learn to flatten them by hand, but it'll take some practice (although the little ladies of Oaxaca make it look so easy!). I use plastic bags to keep the dough from making a sticky mess. A tortilla press makes the job faster and you'll get nice round tortillas each time, but a rolling pin works just as well. Serve with fajitas, as wraps for tacos, or just with some salsa on the side.

MAKES TWELVE 5- TO 6-INCH TORTILLAS

2 cups masa harina

½ teaspoon salt

In a large bowl, combine the masa, salt, and 1½ cups room-temperature water. Keep mixing with your hands until the dough can be formed into a ball.

Divide the dough into 12 pieces that are roughly equal. (The best way to do this is to divide the dough in half, then divide the halves into thirds, and then divide the thirds into halves.)

Heat a nonstick or well-seasoned cast-iron skillet over high heat (see note).

Cut a large resealable plastic bag (see note) so that it opens flat and lay it on your tortilla press. Place a ball of dough in the middle, between the folded sheets of plastic. Press it into a disk. Carefully peel the dough from the plastic bag and place it on the hot skillet. Cook until the tortilla is lightly whitened (about 30 seconds). Flip with a spatula (although I've seen braver women than I just flip them with their bare fingers) and let it cook until lightly whitened, another 30 seconds or so. Remove and place on a platter or plate. Keep the tortillas warm by covering them with a kitchen towel. Repeat until all the tortillas are cooked and ready to serve.

Continued

CORN TORTILLAS *continued*

NOTE: *A nonstick pan or well-seasoned comal or cast-iron skillet keeps you from having to use any oil when cooking the tortillas. You can also use waxed paper in place of a plastic bag when working with the tortilla press.*

VARIATION: *If you don't have a tortilla press, you can use a rolling pin. Place a cut plastic bag on a flat rolling surface. Put a ball of dough in the middle between the 2 sheets of plastic. Roll out with a rolling pin until your tortilla is 5 to 6 inches in diameter. Carefully peel off the plastic bag. Cook as directed above. Don't worry about them being perfectly round. Your tortillas will be a bit rough around the edges at first, but that's part of the homemade charm.*

➤ BAKED TORTILLA CHIPS ➤

(Totopos)

In America, we're used to getting that quintessential basket of chips the moment we sit down at a Mexican restaurant. But in Mexico, tortillas are fried in oil only as a way to use them after they get stale. Tortilla chips were first mass-produced in Los Angeles in the 1940s, but you can easily make them at home. This baked version is not only healthier, but faster, too. Don't worry—just because they're baked doesn't mean that they're not delicious, especially with your favorite salsa or guacamole.

MAKES 4 TO 6 SERVINGS

Twelve 5- to 6-inch Corn Tortillas (page 43 or store-bought)

Vegetable oil spray

Salt

Preheat the oven to 350°F.

Place the tortillas in a stack and cut the rounds into 6 or 8 wedges.

Line two large baking sheets with aluminum foil or parchment paper (just to make clean-up easier). Spread the tortilla wedges out in a single layer on the baking sheets and spray with oil. Turn them over and spray with vegetable oil on the other side. Sprinkle with a bit of salt, to your liking. Then, bake until the chips are crisp, 12 to 15 minutes, rotating the sheets once.

Serve nice and warm. Any leftovers can be stored in an airtight container for about 5 days.

2

SALADS

(Ensaladas)

When people hear the words "Mexican salad," the image that comes up may be the taco salad version, which was so popular when I was growing up in the '80s. The combination of shredded iceberg lettuce and ground beef in a greasy, deep-fried flour tortilla bowl was never my idea of fun. The salads in this chapter are antidotes to those taco salads of fast-food fame. The recipes I've included are lighter and have more of the wonderful flavor combinations that make Mexican cuisine so delicious.

Mexican salads are an excellent way to combine the fire-burning heat of chiles with the cool, crispness of fresh lettuce. The crunchy texture of the white roots in the Jícama Salad (page 52) contrasted with the juicy bite of a tomato mingles well with the mouth-puckering lime juice. It's the surprise of textures, the rich burst of flavors, and the explosion of colors that make salads so fun in Mexican cuisine.

Traditional ensaladas are eaten as side dishes in practically every meal, year-round in Mexico, because of its mild tropical weather. Tossing together fresh vegetables with lime, chili powder, or even cheese makes for a healthful dish to serve alongside meats wrapped in warm tortillas.

"Salad" is a bit of a misnomer in Mexican cuisine because even pico de gallo or guacamole can be considered a "salad" (vegetables tossed together with spices). For the sake of this book, though, I'm using the American way of thinking of salad, as a side dish, appetizer, or second course for a more elaborate meal.

These ensaladas are perfect for a lazy summer afternoon, when you don't want to heat up the kitchen. Whip up any of these easy recipes for a filling lunch or a light dinner. The Carne Asada Salad (page 49), for example, is a meal by itself and perfect for eating before your afternoon siesta. It can be dressed up to serve at a fancy dinner party or just eaten by itself as a delicious treat.

The Festive Corn Salad (page 50) or Cactus Salad (page 51) can be showstoppers for a potluck, or prepared in advance of a party. You'll look like you've been slaving all day in the kitchen, but you didn't even have to turn on the stove!

CARNE ASADA SALAD

(Ensalada con Carne Asada)

This salad is a wonderful way to take leftover carne asada and salsa and transform them into an easy meal. The combination of flavors and textures makes this a fun dish to enjoy any time of year, but if it's warm outside, put on some salsa or merengue music and enjoy a meal alfresco.

MAKES 2 ENTREE OR 4 APPETIZER SERVINGS

- 1 head romaine lettuce, chopped into bite-sized pieces (about 6 cups)
- 1 ripe tomato, diced
- 1 avocado, pitted (see page 57) and sliced
- ½ cup thinly sliced jícama
- 4 green onions, chopped
- ¾ cup olive oil
- ½ cup crumbled cotija cheese
- ½ cup red wine vinegar
- 2 tablespoons freshly squeezed lime juice
- ¼ teaspoon salt
- ⅛ teaspoon freshly ground black pepper
- 1 pound cooked Seasoned Skirt Steak (page 109)
- 1 cup salsa of your choice
- 2 tablespoons toasted pumpkin seeds (optional)

In a large bowl, toss together the lettuce, tomato, avocado, jícama, green onions, olive oil, half the cheese, the vinegar, lime juice, salt, and black pepper. Arrange the salad on a large platter.

Slice the skirt steak into thin strips and arrange on top of the salad. Spoon over the salsa and sprinkle with the remaining cheese. Garnish with the pumpkin seeds, if you wish, before serving.

VARIATION: *If you don't have any leftover carne asada, you can put any cooked meat on top. Try some leftover turkey, shredded chicken, or even some shrimp.*

CORN SALAD

(Ensalada de Maiz)

I had a hard time deciding if this should be classified as a salad or a salsa. I serve it on a bed of lettuce, so it feels more like a salad to me, but if you eat it with some tortilla chips, it can easily be called a salsa. Salsa or salad? You decide. Whatever the case, enjoy it however you like it.

MAKES 4 APPETIZER SERVINGS

3   tablespoons butter

2   cups corn kernels (fresh or thawed from frozen)

1   zucchini, diced

1   red bell pepper, diced

1   ripe tomato, chopped

½   cup chopped fresh cilantro

2   green onions, chopped

⅓   cup olive oil

1   jalapeño pepper, minced

2   tablespoons freshly squeezed lime juice

½   teaspoon salt

½   teaspoon freshly ground black pepper

Green or red leaf lettuce or romaine, for bedding

In a large skillet, melt the butter over high heat. Add the corn and zucchini and sauté until tender, 4 to 5 minutes. Remove from the heat.

Put the corn and zucchini into a large bowl. Add the bell pepper, tomato, cilantro, green onions, olive oil, jalapeño, lime juice, salt, and black pepper and toss.

Serve at room temperature over a bed of lettuce or chill in the refrigerator and serve cold. It'll keep in the fridge overnight if you want to prepare it a day ahead.

⤐ CACTUS SALAD ⤏
(Ensalada de Nopalitos)

I like to get my nopalitos fresh from my neighborhood grocery, with their thorns removed and already cut. If you can't find them that way, though, feel free to substitute the jarred variety and skip the cooking step. Just be sure to rinse them off since they'll be slimy in their cactus juices.

MAKES 6 TO 8 APPETIZER SERVINGS

2   pound nopales, diced or cut into small strips
¼   cup olive oil
2   tablespoons vinegar
2   tablespoons freshly squeezed lime juice
2   garlic cloves, minced
1   teaspoon dried oregano
1   teaspoon salt
1   teaspoon freshly ground black pepper
3   ripe tomatoes, chopped
1   cup coarsely chopped fresh cilantro
½   red onion, thinly sliced
1   serrano pepper, minced
1   firm but ripe avocado, pitted (see page 57) and diced
½   cup crumbled cotija cheese

Bring a large pot of water to a boil over high heat. Add the nopales and boil until softened, about 10 minutes. Rinse three times in cold water until they stop feeling slimy. Drain well and set aside.

In a large bowl, combine the olive oil, vinegar, lime juice, garlic, oregano, salt, and black pepper. Add the nopales, tomatoes, cilantro, onion, and serrano and gently toss. Taste and add a bit more salt, if you think it needs it. Refrigerate for about 15 minutes to let the flavors infuse.

Carefully toss in the avocado and cheese just before serving. Serve cool or at room temperature.

NOTE: *This salad makes a colorful accompaniment to a variety of grilled meats and makes a great filling for tacos and burritos, too. Feel free to omit the serrano if you want your salad to be milder.*

~ JÍCAMA SALAD ~
(Ensalada de Jícama)

Jícamas are underused in cooking—a real shame, since they're such wonderful root vegetables with a crunchy, crispy texture. This salad (which is more akin to a "slaw") highlights the best of the jícama's characteristics and makes a nice side for any fajita or grilled meat.

MAKES 6 TO 8 APPETIZER SERVINGS

- 1 large jícama (about 1½ pounds), peeled and coarsely shredded
- 2 large carrots, coarsely shredded
- 1 large red onion, thinly sliced
- 1 red or yellow bell pepper, julienned
- 1 lime, zested
- ⅓ cup freshly squeezed lime juice (about 3 limes)
- ¼ cup olive oil
- 2 tablespoons honey
- 1 tablespoon ground pure ancho chile
- ¼ cup chopped fresh cilantro
- Salt
- Freshly ground black pepper

In a medium bowl, combine the jícama, carrots, onion, and bell pepper.

In a smaller bowl, whisk together the lime zest, lime juice, olive oil, honey, and ancho. Pour over the vegetables and toss.

Add the cilantro and season with salt and black pepper. Refrigerate for about 30 minutes before serving.

VARIATIONS: *If you want to go with a more fun and varied texture, add a chopped avocado, cut slices of an orange, or even a couple of chopped tomatoes just before tossing.*

AVOCADO SALAD

(Ensalada de Aguacate)

The combination of textures and flavors of this salad makes for a refreshing first course or a nice side to accompany some grilled meats.

MAKES 4 APPETIZER SERVINGS

⅓ cup freshly squeezed lime juice (about 3 limes)

¼ cup olive oil

½ teaspoon salt

½ teaspoon freshly ground black pepper

¼ teaspoon chili powder

2 ripe but firm avocados, pitted (see page 57) and cut into large cubes

2 medium tomatoes, cut into large cubes

1 red onion, chopped

3 medium radishes, thinly sliced

In a small bowl, whisk together the lime juice, olive oil, salt, black pepper, and chili powder.

In a large bowl, combine the avocados, tomatoes, onion, and radishes. Pour in the dressing, toss lightly, and serve immediately.

VARIATIONS: *If you want to make this salad more fun and colorful, you can also add some diced mangoes, papayas, or even some cucumber.*

CHILLED
⇝ BEAN SALAD ⇜
(Ensalada de Habas)

This is the perfect salad for a party, since you can make it up to a day ahead. It can also be served cold, straight out of the refrigerator. It's colorful, spicy, delicious, and you don't have to turn on the stove, which is an added bonus.

MAKES 8 TO 10 APPETIZER SERVINGS

½ cup olive oil

½ cup red wine vinegar

3 tablespoons freshly squeezed lime juice (about 2 limes)

1 tablespoon sugar

1 garlic clove, finely minced

1 teaspoon salt

½ teaspoon freshly ground black pepper

½ teaspoon chili powder

½ teaspoon ground cumin

One 15-ounce can kidney beans, drained

One 15-ounce can garbanzo beans, drained

One 15-ounce can black beans, drained

1 red or green bell pepper, diced

1½ cups frozen corn kernels, thawed (see note)

1 red onion, finely chopped

½ cup chopped fresh cilantro

In a small bowl, whisk together the olive oil, vinegar, lime juice, sugar, garlic, salt, black pepper, chili powder, and cumin.

In a large bowl, combine the beans, bell pepper, corn, onion, and cilantro. Pour in the dressing and toss to coat. Refrigerate until chilled or ready to serve. Serve cold.

NOTE: *To quickly thaw corn kernels, rinse under cold water in a colander and let drain.*

❧ CILANTRO-LIME DRESSING ❧

(Aderezo de Cilantro y Limón)

This brilliant green dressing is especially nice for a light summer green salad, but can be used to top a salad any time of year.

MAKES 2 CUPS

2   tablespoons white vinegar
2   tablespoons freshly squeezed lime juice
1   cup olive oil
1   small bunch fresh cilantro, stems cut
2   green onions
1   garlic clove
1   teaspoon freshly ground black pepper
1   teaspoon salt

Pour the vinegar and lime juice into a food processor or blender. With the processor on low, slowly pour in the olive oil until combined. Add the cilantro, green onions, garlic, black pepper, and salt and process until smooth.

Cover and refrigerate in a tightly closed glass container for up to 5 days, but it's best to use it sooner rather than later.

AVOCADO DRESSING

(Aderezo de Aguacate)

This makes a lovely topping to any salad but can be used as a garnish for grilled fish, to dress up your tacos, or just to drizzle over your enchiladas.

MAKES 1 CUP

1   soft, ripe avocado, pitted (see below)
½   cup chopped fresh cilantro
1   serrano pepper, halved
1   garlic clove, sliced
2   tablespoons olive oil
2   tablespoons freshly squeezed lime juice
¼   teaspoon salt
⅛   teaspoon freshly ground black pepper

Scoop out the flesh of the avocado and place it in a food processor or blender. Add the cilantro, serrano, garlic, olive oil, lime juice, salt, and black pepper and process until puréed.

The dressing will keep in the refrigerator for about 1 day.

~ HOW TO PIT AN AVOCADO ~

Using a good, sharp knife, cut the avocado in half lengthwise, using the pit as a pivot point. Separate the halves. Being careful to keep your hands out of the way, jam the blade of the knife into the pit (the knife should go into the middle of the pit and stick). Rotate the knife around from side to side and the pit comes loose. Hit the handle of the knife on the side of a trash can and the pit should fall right into the garbage. Then you can slice, cube, or scoop out the buttery flesh.

3

SOUPS

(Sopas)

There's something optimistic about a large pot of soup boiling on the stove. It speaks of warm meals, a communal table, and plenty of food to be shared. Steaming cauldrons of soup were ever-present in the *cocinas* (kitchens) of my Latina friends, always ready to be served to a wandering traveler or a surprise visitor on a moment's notice.

At our family's Mexican market, we only had one employee. Arturo was a good-natured man and a former boxer from Mexico. He would teach us boxing moves while we stocked the refrigerator with chilled beers and sodas. He invited us to dinner at his house one night.

His wife had made a big cauldron of menudo and was doling out steaming bowls of it to the huge extended family who lived with them. Their house was so small that we had to take turns eating at the tiny dining table, tucked in the corner of the kitchen. We also took turns holding the baby, washing bowls and spoons, and enjoying the warm humor of the Sandoval family.

Soups are a perfect example of the generosity of the Mexican spirit. Families often had huge copper pots (since copper is so plentiful in Mexico) filled with delicious broth, by-products of boiling meats for hours on the stove. The vegetables and spices grown nearby were added to the pot. This created the variety of regional specialties that are around today.

Often, soups are served in large bowls, with plenty of condiments on the side. Those at the table can add as much of the garnishes as they like, choosing from slices of lime to spoonfuls of Mexican crema, fistfuls of cilantro, or crumbled pieces of tortilla chips. Sometimes, fresh cheese is grated into the bowl, so that the melting goodness can add another dimension of flavor and texture to the soup. These sopas are served as a meal in and of themselves, especially great for a light *cena* (dinner) in the winter.

Unlike in American culture, a small bowl of broth or some kind of soup is often present in many Mexican meals, regardless of the season. Served on the side, eaten as an appetizer course, or just enjoyed as a light meal, soups are the ultimate comfort food.

So, get a pot of water boiling and be ready to ladle out some of your best soups to your friends and family.

➤ AVOCADO-LIME SOUP ≋

(Sopa de Aguacate)

This rich soup is an excellent way to get dinner on the table when you don't feel like turning on the stove. The smoothness of the avocado is a natural balance for the sour lime. The cilantro adds a fun texture and an extra layer of flavor.

MAKES 4 APPETIZER SERVINGS

4   soft, ripe avocados, pitted (see page 57) and peeled

3½ cups cold chicken broth

¼   medium onion

2   tablespoons freshly squeezed lime juice

¼   cup chopped fresh cilantro

1   teaspoon salt

½   teaspoon freshly ground black pepper

4   tablespoons Mexican crema

Place the avocados, broth, onion, lime juice, 2 tablespoons of the cilantro, and the salt and black pepper in a large food processor or blender. (You may have to do this in batches if your blender or food processor is smaller, like mine.) Process until smooth.

Pour into a large bowl, cover, and refrigerate to chill. (At this point, you can put the serving bowls in the refrigerator, too, if you want to get extra fancy.)

Once chilled to your liking, divide the soup among 4 bowls. Top each bowl with 1 tablespoon crema and sprinkle the rest of the cilantro on top before serving.

⇝ LENTIL SOUP ⇜
(Sopa de Lentejas)

The beauty of this soup is that you don't have to soak the lentils beforehand, since they cook up relatively quickly. Although I used chicken broth in mine, you can easily make it vegetarian by using vegetable broth as the base.

MAKES 6 TO 8 APPETIZER SERVINGS

1   tablespoon vegetable or canola oil

1   medium onion, chopped

2   carrots, diced

2   garlic cloves, minced

6   cups chicken broth

One 12-ounce can diced tomatoes, including the juice

1   cup dry brown lentils, rinsed

1   jalapeño pepper, seeded and minced

1   teaspoon ground cumin

1   teaspoon dried oregano

    Salt

    Freshly ground black pepper

    Mexican crema

¼   cup chopped fresh cilantro

Heat the oil in a Dutch oven or large stockpot over medium-high heat. Add the onion, carrots, and garlic, and sauté until the onion is translucent, 3 to 4 minutes. Add the broth, tomatoes and their juice, lentils, jalapeño, cumin, and oregano. Cover and increase the heat to high to bring to a boil. Reduce the heat to medium and continue to cook at a gentle simmer until the lentils are tender, about 20 minutes. Turn off the heat and season with salt and black pepper.

Ladle into individual bowls, topped with a spoonful of crema and some chopped cilantro sprinkled on top.

⤚ SOUP OF THE SEVEN SEAS ⤙

(Caldo de Siete Mares)

I love the romantic name of this soup and love to eat it as a one-dish meal any time of year. I imagine selling all my worldly possessions, buying a boat, and sailing along the Mexican coastline. But since I get too seasick, I'll have to settle for an extra helping of seafood soup, with warm tortillas on the side, and leave the life of sailors and mermaids to my imagination.

MAKES 6 TO 8 ENTREE SERVINGS

1   tablespoon butter or olive oil

2   pounds white fish (catfish, tilapia, etc.), cut into 2- to 3-inch chunks

½   white onion, diced

½   bell pepper, diced

2   tablespoons freshly squeezed lime juice

1   teaspoon salt

1   pound shrimp (shelled or not is up to you)

8   ounces baby octopus

4   ounces squid, sliced

4   ounces shelled mussels

4   small blue crabs, quartered, including shells

1   tomato, diced

1   cup fresh epazote, coarsely chopped

8   cups fish or chicken broth

1   lime, cut into wedges for serving

    Hot sauce for serving

In a large stockpot or Dutch oven, melt the butter over medium-high heat. Add the white fish, onion, bell pepper, lime juice, and salt and toss to coat. Cook, stirring occasionally, until the fish pieces are opaque, about 6 minutes.

Add the shrimp, octopus, squid, mussels, crabs, tomato, and epazote and pour in the broth. Cover and increase the heat to high and bring to a boil. Reduce the heat to medium, keep covered, and let the soup simmer until the seafood is cooked, an additional 15 minutes.

Ladle the soup into large bowls and serve with the lime wedges and hot sauce.

NOTE: *If you can't find epazote, feel free to substitute a bunch of cilantro instead. The flavor will be different, but refreshing, nevertheless.*

❧ TORTILLA SOUP ❧

(Sopa de Tortilla)

Traditional tortilla soup is made with turkey, which is easy to do if you have some leftover bird after Thanksgiving. For everyday meals, I use chicken to make it easier. Some people like to add tomato paste to their broth, but I prefer mine with a cleaner, brighter flavor so that the lime can shine through.

MAKES 6 ENTREE SERVINGS

1   pound boneless, skinless chicken breasts

1   medium onion, diced

2   cups diced zucchini

2   garlic cloves, minced

1   jalapeño pepper, minced

2   bay leaves

1   tablespoon dried or 3 tablespoons
    fresh oregano

½   teaspoon ground cumin

2   large tomatoes, diced

1   cup corn kernels (frozen or canned and drained)

2   tablespoons freshly squeezed lime juice

    Salt

    Freshly ground black pepper

1   lime, cut into wedges for serving

8   ounces queso blanco, crumbled, for serving

½   cup chopped fresh cilantro for serving

1   ripe avocado, pitted (see page 57) and diced
    for serving

    Tortilla chips for serving

Bring 2 quarts of water to a boil in a large pot over high heat. Add the chicken and let simmer for about 20 minutes.

Remove the chicken pieces and set them out on a plate to cool. Add the onion, zucchini, garlic, jalapeño, bay leaves, oregano, and cumin to the water and bring to a boil again. Let simmer over medium-high heat for about 5 minutes.

In the meantime, carefully shred the chicken meat with two forks. Add the chicken, tomatoes, corn, and lime juice to the pot. Season with salt and black pepper. Let boil until the vegetables are heated through, another 5 minutes or so.

Divide the soup among 6 bowls. Serve with the lime wedges, cheese, cilantro, avocado, and tortilla chips on the side, so that each person can add the condiments as they wish.

➤ LIME AND CHICKEN SOUP ➤

(Sopa de Yucatan)

Although this dish originated in the Yucatan, it's popular throughout Mexico. A light soup, wonderful anytime of year, it is especially good when you feel the first signs of a cold coming on. Mexican limes are more akin to Key limes, in that they are smaller, lighter green, and more tart than the larger Persian limes popular in the States. However, any lime will do.

MAKES 4 APPETIZER SERVINGS

1   tablespoon vegetable oil

1½ pounds boneless, skinless chicken breasts, cubed

1   small onion, chopped

2   garlic cloves, minced

6   black peppercorns

1   cinnamon stick

8   whole cloves

1   teaspoon ground cumin

4   cups chicken broth

1   tomato, chopped

1   serrano pepper, finely chopped

1   tablespoon chopped fresh oregano

3   tablespoons freshly squeezed lime juice

¼   teaspoon salt

¼   cup chopped fresh cilantro

4   lime slices

     Tortilla chips for serving

In a large pot with a heavy bottom, heat the vegetable oil over medium-high heat. Add the chicken, onion, garlic, peppercorns, cinnamon, cloves, and cumin. Sauté until the onion turns translucent, 4 to 5 minutes.

Add the broth, tomato, serrano, and oregano and let boil over medium heat for 10 minutes. Remove from the heat and add the lime juice and salt.

Divide into 4 bowls and garnish each with cilantro and a slice of lime. Serve with tortilla chips on the side.

⌒ CHICKEN AND HOMINY SOUP ⌒

(Pozole de Pollo)

Originally from Jalisco, pozole is a stew made from pork and hominy. Although the traditional soup is delicious, it sure isn't a quick meal, since the flavor comes from simmering the pork for hours. So, I've devised a quicker and healthier version with a precooked rotisserie chicken you can pick up at the supermarket. It makes a convenient one-bowl meal for those cold winter nights. And the leftovers taste even better the next day.

MAKES 10 TO 12 APPETIZER SERVINGS

1   whole roasted chicken (4 to 5 pounds)
3   medium onions, 1 quartered and 2 chopped
3   jalapeño peppers, seeded and chopped
4   large garlic cloves, minced
Two 15-ounce cans hominy, drained
1   teaspoon salt
1   tablespoon ground cumin
1   tablespoon chili powder
1   teaspoon dried or 1 tablespoon chopped fresh oregano
½   teaspoon freshly ground black pepper
1   cup chopped fresh cilantro
2   limes, cut into wedges, for serving
4   radishes, sliced, for serving
    Warm Corn Tortillas (page 43 or store-bought), for serving

Shred the chicken and place the meat into a large stockpot or Dutch oven. (It's up to you if you want to add the bones to the soup, since it'll add a little extra dimension of flavor. If you want the soup to be easier to eat, though, discard the bones at this point.) Add 3 quarts of water, the quartered onion, jalapeños, and garlic. Cover and bring to a boil over medium-high heat.

Once boiling, add the hominy, salt, cumin, chili powder, oregano, and black pepper. Reduce the heat slightly, but let the soup continue simmering another 15 to 20 minutes.

Ladle the soup into large bowls and top each with a handful of chopped onion and some cilantro. Serve with the lime wedges, radishes, and warm corn tortillas on the side.

NOTE: *If you have a small family or don't want to make this much soup, just use half the chicken (saving the other half for taco or burrito filling) and halve the remaining ingredients.*

⤳ MEATBALL SOUP ⤳

(Sopa de Albóndigas)

A hearty soup, sopa de albóndigas is great to make as the weather gets colder. It can be an excellent starter, but it's traditionally eaten as a meal with a side of warm tortillas. Serve steaming bowls of it with some hot sauce on the side for those who want to spice it up a bit.

MAKES 8 ENTREE OR 12 APPETIZER SERVINGS

2   tablespoons olive oil

1   large onion, chopped

2   garlic cloves, minced

2   bay leaves

9   cups beef broth

One 28-ounce can diced tomatoes, including the juice

2   large carrots, sliced

1   pound ground beef or pork

1   cup chopped fresh cilantro, plus more for garnish

½   cup uncooked long-grain white rice

1   large egg

½   teaspoon salt

½   teaspoon freshly ground black pepper

½   teaspoon ground cumin

Heat the olive oil in a large, heavy pot over medium-high heat. Add the onion, garlic, and bay leaves and sauté until the onion is translucent, about 5 minutes. Add the broth, tomatoes and their juice, and carrots. Bring to a boil.

Meanwhile, in a medium bowl, combine the ground meat, 1 cup cilantro, rice, egg, salt, black pepper, and cumin. Mix well and pinch off small freeform balls with your fingers or by teaspoonfuls.

When the soup is boiling, add the meatballs. Reduce the heat to medium, cover, and let boil until the meatballs are tender and cooked through, about another 15 minutes. Season with salt and black pepper.

Ladle the soup into large bowls. Garnish with the remaining cilantro and serve immediately.

VARIATION: *You can add about 1½ cups of fresh or frozen peas. Just throw them in during the last 5 minutes of simmering, since they cook up pretty quickly. If you want a lighter soup or to ward off a winter cold, substitute chicken instead of beef broth. You'll still get enough meat flavor from the meatballs.*

⇒ BEEF STEW ⇐

(Carne Guisada)

As a teenager, when I didn't know what to make for dinner, I would just go over and get some stew meat from the carniceria down the street. It was an excuse to practice my bad Spanish on the butcher's son, on whom I had a schoolgirl's crush. I'd throw the meat into a pot and add whatever vegetables were around, along with some tomato sauce. One of our customers taught me how to make their carne guisada, and I've never looked back. My teenage version often included cabbage and potatoes, but here's a more traditional recipe (minus the customary lard). This is delicious with rice and beans or warm tortillas on the side.

MAKES 4 OR 5 ENTREE SERVINGS

1   tablespoon vegetable oil

1½ pounds cubed beef stew meat

1   large onion, diced

½   bell pepper, diced

1   large ripe tomato, diced

One 8-ounce can tomato sauce

2   jalapeño peppers, finely chopped

2   garlic cloves, minced

1   tablespoon chili powder

1   teaspoon salt

½   teaspoon freshly ground black pepper

In a large stockpot, heat the vegetable oil over medium-high heat. Add the stew meat and cook until browned on all sides, about 5 minutes. Add the onion and bell pepper and sauté for an additional 5 minutes.

Add 1 quart of water, the tomato, tomato sauce, jalapeños, garlic, and chili powder, and bring to a boil. Reduce the heat to medium and let cook, covered, on a soft boil for 30 minutes.

Add the salt and black pepper and adjust the seasoning to your taste. Ladle into individual bowls to serve.

~ 4 ~

VEGETABLES AND SIDE DISHES

(Vegetales y Mas)

In traditional Mexican cuisine, the main dishes were meats that had been slow-roasted in a riot of spices. Side dishes, on the other hand, were made from the plants and vegetables that grew wild or were grown in the region.

When I lived in San Miguel de Allende, I always looked forward to the weekly *tianguis*—open markets that traveled around the nearby towns, stopping in each once a week. On Wednesdays, vendors would set up their stalls, laying out baskets of fresh fruits, cartfuls of greens, burlap sacks full of dried chiles, and spices that all called for my attention.

I would ask the vendors what to do with each ingredient. Each one happily cut me pieces of their fresh fruits or let me sample a taste of their soft cheeses, and all of them were generous enough to share their secret recipes.

The women who bought produce from my dad were just as generous in sharing their secrets. They would ask my dad to sell a certain type of vegetable, like wrinkled green chayotes or Mexican zucchini (as opposed to their darker Italian cousins). I would ask how to cook them and not only would the ladies share their recipes, but they would bring me containers of their treasured dishes—warm Aztec Zucchini (page 78) dotted with ripe tomatoes, roasted peppers overstuffed with melting cheese, and dozens of variations on rice and bean dishes.

Sure, chile peppers and tomatoes end up in a lot of the dishes (like the salsas in chapter 1), but fruits and vegetables are just as regular a part of everyday meals. Freshly steamed corn on the cob—Spicy Corn on the Cob (page 81)—is sold slathered in mayonnaise, butter, and chili powder from street carts, while every meal has some sort of vegetable or fruit to accompany the meat and tortillas.

Although traditional cooking involves some frying in lard, modern Mexican dishes can be well adapted to suit vegetarian tastes. Take, for instance, the Vegetarian Quesadilla (page 82). It can easily be made with any seasonal vegetable, sliced and sautéed, then stuffed in a warm tortilla. Roasted Poblano Chiles (page 76) can be cut into strips and used as a filling for enchiladas, tacos, burritos, or substituted in many meat dishes.

The side dishes are as important as the main course, so don't skimp on the beans. Adjust the seasonings in your rice to make it your own and just revel in all the delicious flavors that will make your table that much more inviting.

❧ REFRIED BEANS ❧

(Frijoles Refritos)

When I was living in Mexico, I was a very poor, post-college student. I had taken my last paycheck and moved south of the border to practice guitar, make art, and learn Spanish. It all sounded so lovely and romantic, but the reality was that I was living on frijoles and arroz every day because I couldn't afford to eat anything else. Back then, I had all the time in the world to cook up a big batch of beans. Now, I barely have time to eat a quick dinner before getting back to work, so I came up with this faster version. Traditional refried beans are made with lard, but I've found that bacon grease adds a wonderful flavor.

MAKES 8 TO 10 SIDE-DISH SERVINGS

3   tablespoons bacon grease

½   onion, chopped

2   serrano peppers

2   garlic cloves, minced

Two 15-ounce cans pinto beans, including
    the liquid

¼   cup crumbled cotija cheese

Heat the bacon grease in a large skillet over medium-high heat. Add the onion, serranos, and garlic and sauté until the onion is slightly translucent, 2 to 3 minutes. Remove and discard the serranos (or chop and save to use as topping). Pour in the beans and their liquid and stir. Mash them in the pan with a potato masher or wooden spoon. Keep mashing until you have the texture that you like and stir until all the beans are warmed through.

Serve warm sprinkled with cheese and the chopped serranos, if you like, or use as a filling for your burritos.

NOTE: *The peppers don't make the beans spicy, but add an additional layer of flavor. If you can't find serranos, feel free to substitute a jalapeño.*

VARIATION: *To make a vegetarian version, just substitute olive oil for the bacon drippings.*

BLACK BEANS

(Frijoles Negro)

Because I had eaten so many refried beans in my life and was a temporary vegetarian, my frijoles of choice at one time were black beans. The secret to making beans fast is to start with canned beans. You can use fresh beans, too, of course, but you'll have to soak them in water the night before.

MAKES 4 SIDE-DISH SERVINGS

1   tablespoon olive oil

½   small onion, chopped

1   garlic clove, minced

One 15-ounce can black beans, including the liquid

2   tablespoons freshly squeezed lime juice

1   teaspoon chili powder

1   teaspoon ground cumin

1   tablespoon chopped fresh cilantro

In a large saucepan, heat the olive oil over medium-high heat. Add the onion and garlic and sauté until the onion is translucent, 3 to 4 minutes. Pour in the beans and their liquid, then add the lime juice, chili powder, and cumin and lower the heat to medium. Let simmer, uncovered, until the beans are softened, about 15 minutes. Remove from the heat, sprinkle in the cilantro, and serve.

ROASTED
⤳ POBLANO CHILES ⤳
(Chiles Poblanos)

Poblanos are the most popular chiles in Mexico. They are flavorful, but not too spicy. Roasting them not only helps bring out the flavor, but makes it easier for you to take off their pesky skins. The darker green versions are also called pasillas, and they sometimes can be slightly hotter than the lighter green ones. You can also substitute two Anaheim chiles for each poblano.

MAKES 6 CHILES

6 large poblano or pasilla chiles

Preheat your broiler.

Place the chiles on a baking sheet and place them under the broiler. Broil until parts of the skin are blackened, 5 to 7 minutes. (Don't be alarmed when you hear the skins make popping noises!) With tongs or an oven mitt, carefully turn over the chiles. Broil until parts of the chiles are partially blackened on both sides, another 5 to 7 minutes.

Remove from the oven and place the chiles in a large plastic bag and seal it, letting the chiles steam.

After 5 to 10 minutes, check on the chiles. They should be steamed and the skins should peel off easily. Remove the skins from each chile by peeling with your fingers under cold running water.

At this point, you can stuff the chiles with cheese to make Stuffed Peppers (page 91), slice them to put on sandwiches and burgers, or use strips of them to enhance your quesadillas and enchiladas.

These chiles can be stored in plastic zipper bags or tightly closed glass jars in the refrigerator for about 1 week or frozen for 2 months.

⤳ FRIED POTATOES ⤳

WITH POBLANO CHILES

(Papas Fritas con Rajas)

What would we do without potatoes and chiles? This dish makes the best of both of them, fried up and delicious to be eaten as a side or fillings for tacos.

MAKES 6 TO 8 SIDE-DISH SERVINGS

- 2 tablespoons olive or canola oil
- 2 pounds russet potatoes, peeled and cut into ½-inch thick strips
- 1 large onion, thinly sliced
- 6 Roasted Poblano Chiles (facing page), cut into strips
- 1 teaspoon salt

In a large skillet, heat the oil over medium heat. Add the potatoes and onion and cook until the onion is translucent and the potatoes have softened, about 6 to 8 minutes. Add the roasted chiles and salt and cook until the potatoes have browned, stirring occasionally to keep the vegetables from sticking to the pan.

Serve immediately, nice and hot from the pan.

➤ AZTEC ZUCCHINI ➤

(Colache)

This recipe dates back to the time of the Aztecs, since this is a dish made from the best of the summer harvest including vine-ripened tomatoes, fresh corn, and abundant zucchini. Mexican zucchini are smaller and lighter in color than their Italian cousins, although the flavor is similar. Traditionally, the vegetables were cooked in lard, but I prefer the vegetarian version.

MAKES 6 TO 8 SIDE-DISH SERVINGS

2 tablespoons olive oil
1 tablespoon butter
3 medium zucchini, thinly sliced
1 small onion, diced
3 garlic cloves, sliced
2 ripe tomatoes, diced
1 cup fresh or frozen corn kernels
¼ cup chopped fresh cilantro
½ teaspoon dried or 1½ teaspoons fresh oregano
¼ teaspoon salt
¼ teaspoon freshly ground black pepper
¼ cup shredded cotija cheese

Heat a large skillet over medium heat. Add the olive oil and butter. When the butter is melted, add the zucchini, onion, and garlic and sauté until the vegetables are limp and the onion is slightly translucent, 2 to 3 minutes. Add the tomatoes, corn, cilantro, oregano, salt, and black pepper and simmer until the tomatoes are cooked, 5 minutes more.

Remove from the heat and place in a serving dish. Top with the cheese and serve nice and hot.

FRIED
⤳ CHAYOTE SQUASH ⤳

(Chayotes Fritos)

A hard, green, mild squash, the chayote is another wonderful plant native to Mexico. The beauty of the chayote is that it takes on the flavor of whatever seasoning it's cooked in. Serve on the side of your favorite meat.

MAKES 4 TO 6 SIDE-DISH SERVINGS

2 tablespoons butter
1 tablespoon olive oil
2 medium onions, sliced
2 chayotes, pitted and thinly sliced
2 teaspoons dried or 2 tablespoons chopped fresh oregano
½ teaspoon salt
¼ teaspoon freshly ground black pepper

Heat the butter and olive oil in a large skillet over medium heat. When the butter is melted, add the onions and sauté until they are golden, but not browned, 8 to 10 minutes. Add the chayotes and oregano and sauté for an additional 2 or 3 minutes, until the squash starts to soften. Lower the heat, cover, and cook until the chayote is tender, an additional 10 minutes.

Remove from the heat. Add the salt and black pepper and toss before serving.

VARIATIONS: *If you want to add a variety of flavors and textures, you can include chopped tomatoes, roasted poblanos, zucchini, or other vegetables.*

➤ CORN ON THE COB ➤

(Elotes)

I'm a huge fan of the street food found all over Mexico and have been known to just wander, filling up without setting foot in a restaurant all day. Even street vendors in Los Angeles sell corn freshly roasted, slathered in mayonnaise, and seasoned similarly to this recipe. This is a messy, but delicious, way to enjoy the sweetness of fresh corn with the spicy lime seasoning to balance it.

MAKES 4 SERVINGS

4 ears corn, shucked

¼ cup mayonnaise

2 tablespoons freshly squeezed lime juice

1 teaspoon chili powder

¼ teaspoon ground cumin

⅛ teaspoon salt

¼ cup butter, melted

¼ cup crumbled cotija cheese

Preheat a grill to medium-high heat. Grill the corn until lightly charred and cooked, turning over as needed, 10 to 12 minutes total.

In a small bowl, combine the mayonnaise and lime juice. In a separate bowl, mix together the chili powder, cumin, and salt.

Coat the corn in the butter, then spread the mayonnaise-lime mixture on all sides. Sprinkle with the cheese and the dry seasoning mixture. Eat immediately.

VARIATION: *If you can't find cotija cheese, feel free to substitute grated Parmesan cheese.*

VEGETARIAN

❧ QUESADILLAS ❧

(Quesadillas Vegetarianas)

What goes inside a quesadilla varies from region to region, but all of them are cheese-stuffed tortillas that are cooked until the cheese melts and the tortillas are nice and toasty on the outside. This is a vegetarian version— great for a light lunch or an appetizer for a fancier dinner with a side of guacamole, sour cream, and/or your choice of salsa.

MAKES 3 ENTREE OR 6 APPETIZER SERVINGS

Vegetable oil
1 **medium onion, diced**
1 **bell pepper, cubed**
1 **cup sliced mushrooms**
2 **tomatoes, chopped**
1 **teaspoon chili powder**
Six **7- to 8-inch flour tortillas**
1 **cup shredded queso blanco or crumbled manchego**
½ **cup chopped fresh cilantro**

Heat about 1 tablespoon vegetable oil in a large pan over medium-high heat. Add the onion, bell pepper, and mushrooms and sauté until the onion is translucent and the bell pepper is limp, 3 to 4 minutes. Add the tomatoes and the chili powder and toss. Remove from the heat (the tomatoes will continue to cook a bit in the hot pan).

In a separate pan, heat about 1 teaspoon vegetable oil over medium-low heat. Take one tortilla and place it in the pan. Spoon about one-sixth of the vegetable mix onto half of the tortilla, sprinkle on about 2½ tablespoons cheese and a bit of the cilantro, and fold the tortilla in half. Put another tortilla in the pan and repeat. Now you should have two quesadillas cooking in the pan. Cook until the cheese has melted and the tortillas are crispy and golden brown on both sides, 3 to 4 minutes for each side. Place the quesadillas onto a cutting board and repeat the process (adding a bit more oil to the pan, as necessary) until all the tortillas and filling are used up.

Cut the quesadillas into three wedges each and serve.

➤ MEXICAN RICE ➤

(Arroz à la Méxicana)

A wonderful side dish that works with any number of entrees, this rice is great left over for the next day's meal or for a delicious filling for your burritos. If you like your rice with a spicy kick, go ahead and leave the seeds in the jalapeño. Alternatively, omit the jalapeño altogether if you don't want that extra fire.

MAKES 6 TO 8 SIDE-DISH SERVINGS

2   tablespoons vegetable oil

½   medium onion, chopped

1   jalapeño pepper, finely chopped

3   garlic cloves, chopped

1½ cups uncooked long-grain white rice

1   bay leaf

2½ cups chicken broth

One 14.5-ounce can chopped tomatoes, including the juice

1   teaspoon ground cumin

3 or 4 sprigs cilantro, coarsely chopped (about 2 tablespoons)

In a large saucepan, heat the vegetable oil over medium-high heat. Add the onion, jalapeño, and garlic and sauté until the onion is translucent, 2 to 3 minutes. Add the rice and bay leaf and sauté until the rice becomes opaque and lightly browned, another 4 to 5 minutes.

Slowly (be careful not to splatter!) add the broth, tomatoes and their juice, and cumin and stir. Cover and bring to a boil. Once boiling, turn the heat to low. Let simmer, covered, until the rice is cooked, 20 to 25 minutes.

Fluff the rice and serve hot, sprinkled with the cilantro.

NOTE: *There's no need to add any salt since there's plenty of salt in the canned tomatoes and chicken broth. If you're watching your sodium, I recommend using low-salt varieties.*

⌁ MEXICAN FONDUE ⌁
(Queso Fundido)

Although different from the fondue enjoyed in Europe, this dish highlights the melty goodness of cheese and will make a wonderful starter for your next fiesta.

MAKES 4 OR 5 APPETIZER SERVINGS

3   ounces crumbled chorizo

1   jalapeño pepper, minced

2   cups shredded Oaxacan, asadero, or Chihuahua cheese

1   tablespoon chopped fresh cilantro

    Corn Tortillas (page 43 or store-bought) or tortilla chips for dipping

In a cast-iron skillet, cook the chorizo over medium-high heat until browned, about 5 minutes. Remove the chorizo with a slotted spoon, leaving the fat in the pan. Set the chorizo aside.

Add in the jalapeño and cook, stirring, for about 1 minute, then add the cheese. Reduce the heat to low and stir until all of the cheese is melted, about 3 minutes. Remove from the heat and sprinkle on the chorizo and cilantro.

Serve the fundido—pan and all—with warm tortillas or tortilla chips on the side for dipping.

NOTE: *If you can't find Mexican cheeses in your area, you can substitute Monterey Jack or mozzarella cheese. Also, seed the jalapeño if you want to turn down the fire.*

VARIATION: *To make a vegetarian version, substitute the chorizo with 2 tablespoons olive oil, some chopped mushrooms, and chopped bell peppers. Follow the rest of the directions, as above.*

5

POULTRY AND EGGS

(Aves y Huevos)

When the Spaniards landed on the Yucatan peninsula in 1521, the culinary landscape of the world changed forever. One of the major contributions they brought were chickens, and of course the chickens' eggs. Although the natives had plenty of fowl (quail, pheasant, turkeys, etc.) to choose from, chickens became one of the most popular domesticated animals.

The egg is an economical source of protein and is used in a variety of dishes. From the eggs dropped into *sopa de ajo* (garlic soup) or those cracked to make the creamy dessert flan, these perfect orbs are a staple in Mexican cuisine.

In small markets throughout the country, they're sold by weight. Villagers would bring their own bags and baskets and buy kilos or *medio* (half) kilos of the eggs to make their Ranch-Style Eggs (page 89) or the *huevos con machaca* (eggs and shredded beef) popular in Baja. Hundreds of them are cracked to make the Yucatan wedding dish *higaditos* (which also includes chicken livers), or just a couple of them are hidden in Mexican meat loaf.

The hollowed-out shells are decorated and filled with confetti, to be later cracked onto the heads of partiers during Easter, Christmas, or other festive occasions. Village shamans also pass eggs over the body in a spiritual cleansing ritual called *limpia*.

With all this talk about the egg, let's not forget its producer, the chicken. The wonderful thing about chicken is that it's inexpensive and the meat absorbs the fabulous spices and herbs that it's marinated or cooked in. One of the most popular ways to enjoy chicken is as a filling for enchiladas. I make my Chicken Enchiladas with Green Chile Sauce (page 99) when I don't know how many mouths I have to feed. These delicious birds can also be baked with a creamy chipotle sauce (page 96), smothered in mole sauce (page 97) or rolled into crispy taquitos (page 100).

I've even included a recipe featuring Benjamin Franklin's favorite native bird in the Turkey Chilaquiles dish (page 103), which makes a wonderful (and sinfully easy) after-Thanksgiving breakfast.

The beauty of Mexican cooking is that once you've perfected how to make a dish (e.g., enchiladas), you can make endless combinations to create your own culinary treasures. For instance, you can take most of the beef and pork recipes in Chapter 6 and just substitute chicken to increase your Mexican food repertoire. Never let your chicken be boring again.

⤳ RANCH-STYLE EGGS ⤳

(Huevos Rancheros)

Huevos rancheros are a traditional breakfast and there are as many varieties as there are regions in Mexico. Some make it with beans, roasted chiles, or chorizo. Others like to top it with sour cream, guacamole, or a generous heaping of cheese. I'm providing the basic traditional way to make it, so that you can dress it up however you like.

MAKES 2 ENTREE SERVINGS

Vegetable oil

Four 5- to 6-inch Corn Tortillas (page 43 or store-bought)

4 large eggs

1 cup "Rooster's Beak" Salsa (page 31) or other fresh salsa of your choice

In a frying pan, heat a bit of vegetable oil over medium-high heat. Cook each of the tortillas until they're heated and crisp, about 1 minute on each side. Lay them out two each, slightly overlapping on two large plates.

In the same frying pan, cook the eggs, sunny-side up, two at a time. Place the eggs on top of each pair of tortillas.

In the same pan, heat the salsa until warm through. Spoon half the salsa over each pair of eggs. The warm salsa will cook the tops of the eggs a bit, so let them sit for about 1 minute before serving.

❧ LENTEN EGGS ❧

(Nopales con Huevos)

Eggs and nopales are popular for breakfast, especially during the Lenten season, just before Easter. I discovered this dish after seeing so many señoras buying shredded dried shrimp and cactus together at our family's market. Here's a vegetarian version, which you can enhance by topping with shredded dried shrimp, if you'd like, and a side of warm tortillas.

MAKES 4 ENTREE SERVINGS

1   tablespoon olive oil

1   pound nopales, diced or cut into thin strips

1   medium onion, finely chopped

2   tomatoes, diced

4   serrano peppers, minced

2   garlic cloves, minced

4   large eggs, lightly beaten

1   teaspoon salt

½   teaspoon freshly ground black pepper

4   ounces cotija cheese, crumbled

¼   cup chopped fresh cilantro

Heat the olive oil in a large skillet over medium heat. Add the nopales and cook, covered, until their color darkens, about 10 minutes, stirring occasionally.

Add the onion, tomatoes, serranos, and garlic and cook until the onion is translucent, about 10 minutes more. Add the eggs, salt, and black pepper and stir to scramble and cook the eggs.

Remove from the heat and serve topped with the cheese and cilantro.

⪼ STUFFED PEPPERS ⪻

(Chiles Rellenos)

One of my favorites of all time, I order this dish as a litmus test to tell whether or not a Mexican restaurant will pass muster. The secret to an airy relleno is whipping the egg whites into a big fluffy cloud. The rest is pretty easy and delicious with a side of tortillas, rice, and beans.

MAKES 6 ENTREE SERVINGS

6   Roasted Poblano Chiles (page 76) or 12 canned
8   ounces queso fresco, cut into thin slices
6   large eggs, separated
¾   cup flour
½   teaspoon salt
1   cup canola oil
2   cups Roasted Tomatillo Salsa (page 33) or salsa of your choice

Make a small T-shaped cut at the top of each chile, near the stem. Cut a slit down the full length of each chile and stuff with a few slices of cheese, dividing the cheese equally. Set aside.

In a large bowl, whisk the egg whites with an electric mixer on high speed until stiff peaks form.

In another bowl, whisk the egg yolks with 1 tablespoon of the flour and the salt. Gently fold the yolk mixture into the whites, combining until the color is consistent throughout.

In a medium skillet, heat the canola oil over medium-high heat. The oil is ready if it sizzles when you splash a drop of water into it.

Place the remainder of the flour onto a plate. Carefully dust each chile with the flour and dip each one into the egg batter, coating as evenly as you can. Place the chiles, open-side down, in the oil and cook until golden brown, about 4 minutes on each side. Place on a platter lined with paper towels to drain. Repeat until all the chiles are cooked.

In a medium saucepan, warm the salsa until heated through. Remove from the heat, but leave covered on the stove to stay warm.

Continued

STUFFED PEPPERS *continued*

Place one chile on each plate and pour the salsa over the chiles before serving.

NOTE: *If you don't want your chiles rellenos to be too spicy, remove the ribs and the seeds, since they hold most of the heat of the peppers.*

OVERSTUFFED
❧ CHICKEN SANDWICHES ❧
(Tortas de Pollo)

A torta is a sandwich made with a *telera* (a soft, round roll) or a *bolillo* (a crustier oblong bread, which is soft and white on the inside). The bread can be filled with any type of meat, but I love the chicken version because it's good for you, messy to eat, and so delicious.

MAKES 4 ENTREE SERVINGS

- 2 boneless, skinless chicken breasts (about 1 pound)
- 1 tablespoon freshly squeezed lime juice
- 1 teaspoon chili powder
- 1 teaspoon dried oregano
- ½ teaspoon salt
- ½ teaspoon freshly ground black pepper
- 4 teleras, bolillos, or even large French rolls
  Butter, at room temperature
- 2 cups Refried Beans (page 74) or one 16-ounce can
- ½ cup shredded cotija cheese or 6 ounces queso fresco, sliced
- 1 avocado, pitted (see page 57) and sliced
- 1 cup salsa of your choice
- 2 cups shredded iceberg lettuce

Cut the chicken breasts in half lengthwise, then pound them with a meat tenderizer until flattened to about ½ inch. Sprinkle on both sides with the lime juice, chili powder, oregano, salt, and black pepper. Set aside.

Cut the breads in half and butter all of them on the insides. Heat a large frying pan over medium heat and put in the bread, butter-sides down, to toast. Turn over and toast on the other sides. Remove from the pan and place, butter-sides up, on a platter or large cutting board.

In the same frying pan, sauté the chicken over high heat until cooked through, about 10 minutes total.

While the chicken is cooking, heat the refried beans in a microwave-safe bowl in the microwave for 1 minute. Stir the beans, then microwave for an additional 30 seconds or until the beans are heated through. Spread the beans on the bottom halves of the bread, then layer the cheese on each of the bean-covered breads.

Place one piece of chicken onto each of the sandwiches. Top with slices of avocado, spoonfuls of salsa, and generous piles of lettuce. Cover with the top bread halves, cut in half, and serve.

CHICKEN BAKED IN
~ CREAMY CHIPOTLE SAUCE ~

(Pollo en Crema de Chipotle)

The crema is a wonderful counterbalance to the smoky spiciness of the chipotle peppers. Feel free to use any cut of chicken, but I prefer to use dark meat for this dish because it works better with the sauce. Crema can be found in the refrigerated section of most Latino groceries. Serve this dish with a side of warm tortillas and perhaps a side of rice or salad.

MAKES 6 ENTREE SERVINGS

1 tablespoon butter

12 pieces bone-in, skinless chicken legs and thighs

4 garlic cloves, sliced

One 15-ounce jar Mexican crema

4 chipotle peppers in adobo sauce, including the sauce

1 teaspoon salt

Preheat the oven to 400°F.

In a large frying pan, melt the butter over high heat and add the chicken and garlic, turning over once to brown the chicken on both sides, about 4 minutes on each side. Remove the pan from the heat.

In a food processor or blender, combine the crema, chipotles, and salt, and process until smooth.

If your frying pan has an oven-safe metal handle, you can leave the chicken in it. If not, move the chicken and garlic to a baking dish. Pour the sauce over the chicken and bake until the meat is cooked through, about 30 minutes.

Serve immediately.

NOTE: *Feel free to add (or remove) 1 or 2 peppers to the sauce, based on your spice tolerance.*

❧ CHICKEN WITH MOLE SAUCE ❧

(Pollo en Mole Poblano)

It can take several hours to make a traditional mole poblano. For those of us who don't have the luxury of time or the molcajete to do it right, we can still have the delicious taste of this classic brown mole without the hassle. You can find a variety of prepared moles sold in the deli section of many Mexican markets or jars of mole in the spice aisle of many supermarkets. Varieties of mole can even be mail-ordered, if you live in a remote area. Serve the chicken with a side of Mexican Rice (page 83) and beans.

MAKES 6 ENTREE SERVINGS

3   boneless, skinless chicken breasts
    (about 1½ to 2 pounds)
8   ounces mole poblano paste

Cut the chicken breasts in half lengthwise so that you have six pieces.

Put the chicken and 3 cups of water in a heavy saucepan and bring to a boil over high heat. Reduce the heat and let it simmer, covered, until the chicken cooks through, about 15 minutes. Put the chicken on a plate and keep covered near the stove to stay warm.

Turn the heat to medium. Add the mole paste to the chicken broth and stir until heated through and thickened, about 10 minutes.

Divide the chicken among 6 plates. Generously pour the mole sauce over each chicken piece and serve.

⤜ CHICKEN ENCHILADAS ⤛

WITH GREEN CHILE SAUCE

(Enchiladas de Pollo con Salsa Verde)

The tangy green sauce here complements the mild cheese and chicken flavors well. Even the pickiest of kids will gobble up this dish, so it makes for an easy weeknight meal. It's best to soften the tortillas first by frying them in a little oil, so I developed a faster way to heat them.

MAKES 6 ENTREE SERVINGS

Twelve 5- to 6-inch Corn Tortillas (page 43 or store-bought)

    Cooking oil spray

    Vegetable oil

2 **boneless, skinless chicken breasts (about 1 pound), sliced into small strips**

1 **teaspoon dried oregano**

½ **teaspoon salt**

½ **teaspoon freshly ground black pepper**

1 **onion, sliced**

1 **green or red bell pepper, sliced**

12 **ounces queso blanco, grated**

One 28-ounce can green chile enchilada sauce

Preheat the oven to 400°F. Coat each tortilla on both sides with cooking oil spray. Place the tortillas on a foil-lined baking sheet and bake for 5 minutes to soften them. Remove from the oven and set aside. Leave the oven on, but lower the heat to 350°F.

Heat about 1 tablespoon vegetable oil in a large skillet over high heat. Add the chicken, oregano, salt, and black pepper, and sauté until the meat is opaque on the outsides, about 5 minutes. Add another tablespoon of oil, then add the onion and bell pepper slices and sauté until the chicken is cooked through, another 3 to 4 minutes. Remove from the heat and pour the chicken mixture into a large bowl. Add two-thirds of the queso blanco and 1 cup of the enchilada sauce and toss together.

Coat a 9-by-13-inch baking dish with vegetable oil spray. Lay all of the tortillas out flat. Spoon the filling into the middle of each tortilla, dividing it evenly. Fold each tortilla over into thirds and lay the filled enchilada, seam-side down, in the baking dish. Repeat until all of the tortillas are done and the baking dish is full.

Pour over the remaining enchilada sauce and sprinkle with the remaining cheese. Bake until the sauce is bubbling and the cheese is melted, about 15 minutes. Remove from the oven and serve two to each diner.

➥ CHICKEN TAQUITOS ➥

(Taquitos de Pollo)

Taquitos (which means "little tacos") are a popular *antojito* (appetizer) in Mexico. They are made of corn tortillas with a little bit of filling, that are rolled up into a fat cigar shape. The subsequent deep-frying keeps the tortillas rolled, and gives them that delicious crispy texture. Here's a simple recipe with chicken that makes a wonderful after-school snack for the kids, with some Chunky Avocado Dip (page 36) and/or your choice of salsa on the side.

MAKES 24 TAQUITOS

2 cups shredded cooked chicken

1 cup crumbled cotija cheese

½ medium onion, finely diced

One 4-ounce can diced green chiles, well drained

½ teaspoon dried oregano

½ teaspoon salt

¼ teaspoon freshly ground black pepper

Vegetable oil

Twenty-four 5- to 6-inch Corn Tortillas (page 43 or store-bought)

In a large bowl, combine the chicken, cheese, onion, chiles, oregano, salt, and black pepper and toss to mix.

In a heavy skillet, heat 2 tablespoons of vegetable oil over medium-high heat. Cook the tortillas, one at a time, in the hot oil until they are soft and limp, about 5 seconds on each side. Stack the tortillas between layers of paper towels, keeping them warm by covering with a kitchen towel.

Spoon about 2 tablespoons of the chicken mixture in a line across the lower third of each tortilla and roll them up tightly. Lay seam-side down on a plate or platter.

In the same heavy skillet, add oil to about ½ inch deep and heat over medium-high heat. Fry the taquitos, seam-sides down (five or six at a time, depending on the size of your pan). Cook until golden brown all over, about 2 minutes on each side. Drain on a paper towel–lined plate or platter and continue until all the taquitos are cooked.

Serve warm.

VARIATION: *If you're watching your health and don't want to deep-fry these, bake them instead. Preheat the oven to 425°F. While the oven is heating, line a baking sheet with foil and coat with a light spritz of oil. Lay the taquitos, seam-sides down, on the sheet, making sure they don't touch each other. Coat the taquitos with cooking oil spray and bake until crispy and the ends start turning golden brown, 15 to 20 minutes.*

CHICKEN TACOS

(Tacos al Carbon de Pollo)

Perfect for a light summer lunch, this is a healthful and delicious way to beat the heat. If you don't want to bother with a grill, you can cut the chicken into strips, then pan-fry in a skillet.

MAKES 6 ENTREE SERVINGS

2   tablespoons freshly squeezed lime juice

2   tablespoons olive oil

2   garlic cloves, minced

1   teaspoon ground cumin

1   teaspoon chili powder

1   teaspoon dried oregano

½   teaspoon salt

¼   teaspoon freshly ground black pepper

1½ pounds boneless, skinless chicken thighs or breasts, butterflied or tenderized

Twelve 5- to 6-inch Corn Tortillas (page 43 or store-bought)

1   cup grated queso fresco

1   avocado, pitted (see page 57) and sliced

2   cups chopped romaine lettuce

    Mexican crema

    Salsa of your choice for serving

In a medium bowl, whisk together the lime juice, olive oil, garlic, cumin, chili powder, oregano, salt, and black pepper. Add the chicken and make sure all of the chicken is well coated. Cover and refrigerate to marinate for at least 30 minutes or overnight.

Preheat a grill to medium-high. Grill the chicken until it is cooked through, 8 to 10 minutes total. Remove from the grill and cut into strips or cubes.

Heat the tortillas over the grill or in the microwave. Fill the tortillas with chicken, cheese, avocado, and lettuce. Serve two tacos per person with a bit of crema and salsa on the side.

➤ CHILAQUILES ➤

(Chilaquiles de Pavo)

Chilaquiles are the ultimate in Mexican comfort food. It's what moms and *abuelas* (grandmothers) make for you for breakfast when they have some old tortillas and some leftover salsa. Usually eaten for breakfast with eggs and a side of nopalitos, chilaquiles are great as a quick lunch or an afternoon snack, as well. The staler the tortillas, the better—so that they don't get so soggy. Use kitchen shears to cut them easily.

MAKES 4 ENTREE SERVINGS

Vegetable oil

Twelve 5- to 6-inch Corn Tortillas (page 43 or store-bought), cut into 8 wedges

¼ teaspoon salt

3 cups Roasted Tomatillo Salsa (page 33) or Red Enchilada Sauce (page 37)

3 or 4 sprigs fresh epazote (optional)

2 cups shredded cooked turkey, warmed

2 cups crumbled cotija or queso fresco

½ red onion, chopped

1 avocado, pitted (see page 57) and sliced

¼ cup chopped fresh cilantro

4 tablespoons Mexican crema

Pour the vegetable oil to a depth of about ⅛ inch in a large frying pan and place over high heat. When the oil is hot, add the tortilla pieces and fry until golden brown. Remove the tortillas and place them on a plate lined with paper towels. Sprinkle with the salt.

Remove any brown bits of tortilla from the pan, but leave the oil. Bring the pan back up to high heat. Add the salsa and epazote sprigs (if using) and let cook until bubbling. Add the tortilla wedges and toss to coat.

Divide among 4 plates and top with the turkey, cheese, onion, and avocado. Sprinkle the cilantro on top and add a tablespoon of crema to each plate before serving.

≫ 6 ≪

BEEF AND PORK
(Carne de Res y Cerdo)

When I was fifteen, I walked to the carniceria down the street from our Mexican market and bought some stew meat for dinner. The next day, I returned for carne asada, and pork the following day. My mom wondered why I had a sudden interest in beef stews and pork butts, but my dad was just happy that I was making him meat every night. That was the summer when I had a crush on the boy at the carniceria and perfected my carne asada recipe.

Although my schoolgirl's crush didn't last more than a season, my love for Mexican meat dishes grew over the years. I still swoon over spicy meats doused in lime, and shredded pork made red with mouth-watering seasoning.

So, when I first moved to Mexico, I was delighted to find out that Mexicans traditionally ate four to five times a day. What wonderful opportunities for a hungry girl to sample all the delicious flavors from many regions! Although most of the day was composed of small bites, the main meal was at midday.

Shops and stalls close around two o'clock in the afternoon. Casual tourists mistake the time for siesta and think that everyone is going home for their afternoon naps. In fact, the owners and workers have all gone home to enjoy the big meal of the day with their families.

Much like American dinner as the main meal, *comida* is eaten around two to three in the afternoon, as a relaxed affair consisting of several courses. The central course, *guisado*, is usually a meat or seafood dish.

Hunks of meat are rubbed in spices and roasted or boiled for hours to release the deep flavors. They are eaten with fresh tortillas, perhaps some beans and/or rice on the side, and plenty of salsa to go around.

In our daily lives, we don't have the luxury of a slow afternoon meal, nor the time to cook meat for hours. But that doesn't mean that we have to sacrifice flavor. We can still enjoy the aromatic spices and gloriously rich complexities of the dishes.

I've filled the following pages with simplified recipes that don't compromise flavor, but still help you get dinner on the table after a long workday. Recipes like Beef Enchiladas with Red Sauce (page 108) can even be doubled, so that you can freeze portions for later meals or to take to lunch.

Dishes like the Spicy Pork Rubbed with Achiote Paste (page 116) or the Seasoned Skirt Steak (page 109) showcase the seasonings and the flavors of the meat. And you can even have plenty of leftovers to be used as taco or burrito fillings for later meals.

⤜ SHREDDED BEEF ⤛

(Machaca)

Traditional *machaca* is the Mexican equivalent of beef jerky. The beef is marinated, cooked, then dried. When you're ready to eat, the meat is pounded into shreds and cooked in a broth. Shredded beef, even when not dried, is also called machaca and can be cooked with potatoes or served over eggs for a hearty breakfast. Here's an easy recipe with plenty of meat for leftovers.

MAKES 5 CUPS

2 tablespoons vegetable oil

3 pounds chuck roast or boneless beef shoulder, cut into 3-inch chunks

1 onion, diced

1 bell pepper, diced

1 jalapeño pepper, minced

4 garlic cloves, minced

¼ cup freshly squeezed lime juice (about 2 limes)

1 tablespoon dried oregano

1 tablespoon ground cumin

1 tablespoon chili powder

¼ cup chopped fresh cilantro

Heat the vegetable oil in a large stockpot over medium-high heat. Sear the beef until it's browned on all sides, 6 to 8 minutes. Add the onion, bell pepper, jalapeño, and garlic and sauté until fragrant, an additional 2 to 3 minutes. Add 2 quarts of water, the lime juice, oregano, cumin, and chili powder and bring to a boil. Reduce the heat to medium and cook at a rolling boil for 1 hour.

Strain the broth, reserving 1 cup and saving the rest for another use.

In a large bowl, carefully shred the meat with two forks. Pour in the 1 cup broth, add the cilantro, and toss.

Use as a filling for tacos, burritos, tamales, tostadas, flautas, or whatever your heart desires.

NOTE: *Leftover machaca can be frozen for several weeks. Divide it into individual portions in plastic zipper bags and store for quick meals later.*

➤ BEEF FLAUTAS ≺

(Flautas de Carne)

Flautas are aptly named tortilla "flutes" that are rolled up with a variety of delicious fillings. Usually the difference between flautas and taquitos is that flautas are made with larger flour tortillas, so are a bit longer than their taquito cousins, which are made from smaller corn tortillas. They are both delicious just the same, with your choice of Chunky Avocado Dip (page 36) or salsa on the side.

MAKES 12 FLAUTAS

2 pounds lean ground beef or Shredded Beef (page 106)
1 medium onion, chopped
2 garlic cloves, minced
2 tablespoons chili powder
1 teaspoon ground cumin
1 teaspoon salt
½ teaspoon freshly ground black pepper
   Vegetable oil
Twelve 10- or 12-inch flour tortillas

In a large dry skillet over high heat, cook the beef, onion, and garlic until all of the meat is cooked, about 20 minutes. Add the chili powder, cumin, salt, and black pepper and combine. Drain the liquid and set aside.

In a clean heavy skillet, heat 2 tablespoons vegetable oil over medium-high heat. Cook the tortillas, one at a time, in the hot oil, until they are soft and limp, about 5 seconds on each side. Stack the tortillas between layers of paper towels, keeping them warm by covering with a kitchen towel.

Spoon about 2 tablespoons of the beef mixture in a line across the lower third of each tortilla and roll them up tightly, sealing closed with toothpicks. Lay seam-side down on a plate or platter.

In the same heavy skillet, add oil to about ½ inch deep and heat over medium-high heat. Fry the flautas, seam-sides down (five or six at a time, depending on the size of your pan). Cook until slightly golden, about 2 minutes on each side. (Remember that flautas are better on the softer side.) Drain on a paper towel-lined plate or platter and continue until all the flautas are cooked.

Remove the toothpicks and serve warm.

~ BEEF ENCHILADAS ~
WITH RED SAUCE
(Enchiladas de Carne con Salsa Roja)

The first time I had beef enchiladas, I was a young immigrant having lunch at school. The Los Angeles Unified School District served these ridiculously greasy beef enchiladas, drowned in tomato sauce and covered in an unidentifiable orange cheese. Luckily for me, I had real beef enchiladas a couple of years later and realized that my first experience barely counted. This recipe is enough to feed a good-size family, with your choice of sides, but feel free to double the recipe and freeze for later.

MAKES 6 ENTREE SERVINGS

Twelve 5- or 6-inch Corn Tortillas (page 43 or store-bought)

Cooking oil spray

Vegetable oil

1½ pounds ground beef or Shredded Beef (page 106)

1   tablespoon chili powder

1   tablespoon fresh or 1 teaspoon dried oregano

1   teaspoon ground cumin

½   teaspoon salt

½   teaspoon freshly ground black pepper

1   onion, chopped

1   green or red bell pepper, sliced

12 ounces queso blanco, grated

Red Enchilada Sauce (page 37) or one 28-ounce can red enchilada sauce

Preheat the oven to 400°F. Coat each tortilla on both sides with cooking oil spray. Place the tortillas on a foil-lined baking sheet and bake for 5 minutes to soften them. Remove from the oven and set aside. Leave the oven on, but lower the heat to 350°F.

Heat about 1 tablespoon of vegetable oil in a large skillet over high heat. Add the beef, chili powder, oregano, cumin, salt, and black pepper, and sauté until the meat is lightly browned, 6 to 7 minutes. Add the onion and bell pepper and sauté until the onion is translucent, 3 to 4 minutes. Put the beef mixture into a large bowl. Add two-thirds of the queso blanco and 1 cup of the sauce and toss together.

Coat a 9-by-13-inch baking dish with cooking oil spray. Lay all of the tortillas out flat. Spoon the filling into the middle of each tortilla, dividing it evenly. Fold each tortilla over in thirds and lay the filled enchilada, seam-side down, in the baking dish. Repeat until all of the tortillas are used and the baking dish is full.

Pour over the remaining sauce and sprinkle with the remaining cheese. Bake until the cheese is melted and the sauce is bubbling, 15 minutes. Remove from the oven and serve two per diner.

SEASONED

⤳ SKIRT STEAK ⤶

(Carne Asada)

Here is a recipe I perfected the summer I was fifteen years old. If you're lucky enough to have your own neighbor-hood carniceria, you can easily get the right cut of meat. If you don't have a Mexican butcher nearby, you can substitute thinly sliced New York steak. No need to tenderize the meat because the marinade will do that for you. Serve with your choice of salsa, chopped cilantro, and warm tortillas.

MAKES 5 OR 6 ENTREE SERVINGS

⅓ cup freshly squeezed lime juice (about 3 limes)

4 garlic cloves, minced

1 tablespoon fresh or 1 teaspoon dried oregano

1 tablespoon chili powder

1 teaspoon ground cumin

Salt

Freshly ground black pepper

3 pounds skirt steak

In a small bowl, combine the lime juice, garlic, oregano, chili powder, and cumin. Season with salt and black pepper. Place the meat in a shallow baking pan or large plastic zipper bag. Pour the marinade over the meat, making sure it is completely coated. Marinate for at least 4 hours or overnight in the refrigerator.

Preheat a grill to high heat or turn on the broiler. Barbecue or broil the beef until it is browned completely on both sides, 8 to 10 minutes total.

Serve immediately.

VARIATIONS: *Some of my friends add Italian dressing and/or beer to marinate the meat, too. I know it sounds weird, but both make the beef tender and add a different flavor. Any kind of beer will do, but why not choose a Mexican beer? Then, you can enjoy the leftover bottles with your meal.*

⤳ STEAK FAJITAS ⤳
(Fajitas de Carne)

Fajitas are usually made with skirt steak and served sizzling hot with onions and peppers. I'm providing a beef version, but it can also be made with chicken, shrimp, or even firm tofu if you want a vegetarian option. Experiment with your favorite fillings and enjoy with salsa, Chunky Avocado Dip (page 36), some more chopped cilantro, and/or Mexican crema.

MAKES 4 OR 5 ENTREE SERVINGS

¼ cup chopped fresh cilantro

3 tablespoons olive oil

2 tablespoons freshly squeezed lime juice

1 serrano pepper, seeded and finely chopped

2 garlic cloves, minced

1 teaspoon ground cumin

1 pound skirt or flank steak

1 large onion, sliced in half, then cut into strips (with the grain)

2 large bell peppers, cut into strips lengthwise

Tortillas for serving

In a bowl, combine the cilantro, 2 tablespoons of the olive oil, the lime juice, serrano, garlic, and cumin. Add the steak and toss until coated. Marinate in the refrigerator for 15 minutes or overnight.

Heat the remaining 1 tablespoon of oil in a large cast-iron pan over high heat. Add the steak, frying on each side to your desired doneness (if you want it cooked medium-rare, cook for about 3 minutes on each side). Remove the meat from the pan and set aside on a cutting board, while the vegetables cook.

Reduce the heat to medium-high, add the onion and bell peppers, and sauté until the onion is translucent, about 5 minutes. Remove from the heat but leave the vegetables in the pan.

Cut the meat against the grain into thin slices. Put it back in the pan with the vegetables and serve immediately with warm tortillas.

GRILLED
➤ TAMPICO-STYLE STEAK ➤
(Carne à la Tampiqueña)

Tampiqueña beef refers to a type of carne asada (a thin steak) cooked and served in the style of Tampico, a city in the state of Tamaulipas in the Gulf of Mexico. A relatively modern town, this "city of otters" (that's what its name means) originated this specific type of steak. It's usually served with warm tortillas and a cheese enchilada on the side.

MAKES 6 ENTREE SERVINGS

6   thin sirloins, about ¼-inch thick

2   tablespoons freshly squeezed lime juice

2   garlic cloves, minced

1   teaspoon salt

½   teaspoon freshly ground black pepper

2   medium onions, cut into thick slices
    (3 slices per onion)

6   thick slices queso asadero

2   Roasted Poblano Chiles (page 76),
    cut into strips

2   avocados, pitted (see page 57) and sliced

2   limes, cut into wedges
    Salsa of your choice

Season the meat with the lime juice, garlic, salt, and black pepper and let marinate while the grill is heating.

Heat an oiled grill to high heat. Grill the onions until golden and limp, about 3 minutes on each side. Put a slice of onion onto each plate. Then, quickly cook the steak, until the edges are browned. Flip over just once, cooking for 6 minutes total. Lay the steaks on each plate with the onions.

Grill the cheese quickly and carefully, making sure it doesn't burn. Place a slice of cheese on each plate, then arrange the chile strips, avocados, and lime wedges on each plate.

Serve immediately topped with salsa.

VARIATION: *If you don't want to bother with a grill, you can cook the steaks in a broiler. Just preheat your broiler to high and cook for about 3 minutes on one side. Then, turn the steaks over, top each piece with a slice of cheese and onion, and broil on the other side. Voila!*

⤳ BREADED STEAK ⤳

(Milanesa)

Popular throughout Latin America, breaded steak not only makes a wonderful dinner but is a great filling for tortas (see page 94). This dish can easily be made with pounded chicken breasts or veal, as well. Serve with freshly squeezed lime juice and a side of salad, tortillas and salsa, or rice and beans.

MAKES 8 ENTREE SERVINGS

Vegetable oil
2 large eggs
½ cup milk
1 cup dried bread crumbs
¼ cup grated Parmesan cheese
2 garlic cloves, minced
2 teaspoons dried oregano
¼ teaspoon salt
⅛ teaspoon freshly ground black pepper
2 pounds beef sirloin or round steaks, cut into ¼-inch slices

Pour vegetable oil to a depth of about ½ inch in large skillet and place over medium-high heat.

While the oil is heating, whisk together the eggs and milk in a shallow bowl.

In a separate bowl or dish, combine the bread crumbs, cheese, garlic, oregano, salt, and black pepper.

Dip the steak slices first in the egg mixture, then coat in the bread crumb mixture. Carefully slip the meat into the hot oil and cook until lightly browned, 2 to 3 minutes on each side. Drain on plates lined with paper towels. Repeat until all the meat is cooked.

Serve immediately.

⇜ PORK TOSTADAS ⇝

(Tostadas de Cerdo)

Tostadas are another ingenious dish created from stale tortillas. Deep-frying the tortillas helps enhance their flavor and makes them a vehicle for adding on whatever topping you want. It's a messy and thoroughly satisfying meal— great for an easy lunch or dinner. This is my pork version that you can pile as high as you like.

MAKES 4 ENTREE SERVINGS

1   pound ground pork

1   medium onion, chopped

2   garlic cloves, minced

2   tablespoons freshly squeezed lime juice

1   tablespoon chili powder

1   teaspoon ground cumin

1   teaspoon salt

One 16-ounce can refried beans

8   tostada shells

2   cups shredded cotija or Cheddar cheese

1   cup "Rooster's Beak" Salsa (page 31) or salsa of your choice

4   cups chopped or shredded lettuce

2   avocados, pitted (see page 57) and diced

1   cup Mexican crema

Heat a large skillet over medium-high heat. Brown the pork, onion, and garlic. Then, add the lime juice, chili powder, cumin, and salt. Cover and let cook, stirring occasionally, until the pork is cooked through, about 10 minutes.

In a microwave-safe bowl, microwave the refried beans until heated through, 1 to 1½ minutes. Spread some refried beans on each of the tostada shells. Place two tostadas on each plate. Top with the cooked pork mixture, cheese, salsa, lettuce, avocados, and a dollop of crema.

∾ SPICY PORK ∾
RUBBED WITH ACHIOTE PASTE
(Cochinita Pibil)

Traditional cochinita pibil is made by slow-roasting pork, wrapped in plantain leaves, for several hours in a low-heat oven. As much as I love the slow cooking, I also like to enjoy the flavors without waiting for hours for the pork to cook. I've devised a quick way to make this dish without losing any of the flavor. Serve with warm tortillas or rice and your choice of salsa.

MAKES 4 TO 6 ENTREE SERVINGS

3   tablespoons Achiote Paste (page 39)
2   garlic cloves, minced
2   pounds boneless pork butt or shoulder, cut into small chunks
2   onions, sliced
1   cup freshly squeezed orange juice
½   cup red wine vinegar
2   tablespoons freshly squeezed lime juice
1   habanero pepper, seeded and chopped (careful with this!)

In a small bowl, combine the achiote paste with the garlic and rub the paste all over the pork, until the meat is covered. Heat a large skillet over high heat. Add the pork and onions and sauté until they are browned, 6 to 8 minutes.

In a large bowl, combine the orange juice, vinegar, lime juice, and habanero. Pour over the cooked pork mixture and cover to simmer over medium heat until cooked through, 15 minutes, stirring occasionally.

Serve immediately.

7

FISH AND SHELLFISH

(Pescados y Mariscos)

In Mexican coastal towns, fish, shellfish, and other treasures of the sea are abundant, especially during the cooler months of the year. This works out great for the end of winter—the start of the Lenten season, when the largely Catholic country switches to eating fish on Fridays. But having to eat fish on Fridays in Mexico is more of a treat than a penance.

The *pescadores* (fishermen) push their boats out in the early morning and return as the sun sets, their nets heavy with the fruits of their labor. Seafood stalls and restaurants line the streets along the coast, waiting for those water creatures to be hauled in from the sea. Even inland, fresh seafood is plentiful, since fishmongers drive the seafood inside large Styrofoam coolers loaded in the back of run-down pickup trucks and wagons.

Nothing beats pulling up at a Mexican seafood stand (the stand itself made from an old boat that's been turned upside down into a makeshift counter). I didn't always know the name in English of some of the shellfish, but the nice vendors would crack open the wet shells and show me the meaty flesh inside.

When it's fresh and raw, white fish, shrimp, octopus, or even lobster can be turned into Ceviche (page 122), all "cooked" in the lime juice generously squeezed over their tender bits. Topping it up with some hot sauce, diners scoop all that goodness onto a tostada. It's fun to watch everyone try to get the whole mess into their mouths without dripping juices down their chins and before the tostada falls apart.

Because of its geographic location, Mexico is blessed with miles and miles of coastline. The Baja Peninsula, one of the longest peninsulas in the world, created the mild waters of the Gulf of California, while still benefiting from the vastness of the Pacific Ocean. It's perfect for gathering shrimp, fishing out lobsters, and digging clams from their sandy hiding places when the tide goes out.

It's no wonder that the people in the coastal towns are so relaxed and happy. They gather the seafood, plentiful in the nearby waters, and the happy fish eventually make their way onto your plate and into your even happier belly.

➤ SHRIMP COCKTAIL ⤙
(Coctel del Camarón)

A popular street food in Veracruz and Mexico's other coastal towns, shrimp cocktail makes a refreshing summer snack. I prefer to eat it with tortilla chips, but more often than not, it's served with Saltine crackers, which tend to get a bit soggy from the soupy sauce.

MAKES 8 APPETIZER SERVINGS

¾ cup ketchup

¼ cup Mexican hot sauce

2 pounds medium shrimp, cooked, peeled, and deveined

½ medium onion, finely chopped

½ cup chopped fresh cilantro

2 tablespoons freshly squeezed lime juice

1 garlic clove, minced

1½ cups tomato-clam juice

1 ripe, but still firm avocado

In a small bowl, combine the ketchup and hot sauce and set aside.

In a medium bowl, toss together the shrimp, onion, cilantro (leave a bit to use as garnish later, if you wish), lime juice, garlic, and about ¾ cup of the ketchup mixture. Add the tomato-clam juice and mix well. Cover and refrigerate until chilled and the flavors have had a chance to soak in (at least a couple of hours or preferably overnight).

Pit and slice the avocado. Divide the shrimp cocktail into small bowls and top each with avocado slices, a dollop of the remaining ketchup mixture and a bit of cilantro, if you wish, before serving.

VARIATIONS: *If you want to add some kick to this dish, add a bit of finely chopped jalapeño pepper. You can also substitute a vegetable juice cocktail in place of the tomato-clam juice, should you desire.*

≻ CEVICHE ≺

This is a wonderful way to enjoy fresh fish in the summertime; the acid of the lime juice "cooks" the fish while it marinates. Although you can add all kinds of seafood to this dish (shrimp, octopus, squid, etc.), I've kept this recipe simple with just fish. Feel free to experiment with your favorite fresh seafood.

MAKES 4 TO 6 APPETIZER SERVINGS

1   pound sushi-grade raw white fish (sea bass, halibut, etc.)

1   cup freshly squeezed lime juice (about 10 limes)

1   garlic clove, minced

2   ripe tomatoes, diced

1   cup roughly chopped fresh cilantro

1   avocado, pitted (see page 57) and cubed

½   cup chopped red onion

4   serrano peppers, chopped

½   teaspoon salt

In a glass or metal bowl, toss together the fish, lime juice, and garlic. Let marinate in the refrigerator for about 30 minutes. In the meantime, prepare the other ingredients.

After 30 minutes, remove the bowl from the refrigerator and add the tomatoes, cilantro, avocado, onion, serranos, and salt.

Serve immediately. Ceviche is best eaten the day it's made so the fish doesn't break down too much from the acid.

NOTE: *If you plan on serving the ceviche later, combine all of the ingredients except the avocado and refrigerate. Add the avocado just before serving.*

❧ VERACRUZ-STYLE FISH ❧

(Pescado Veracruzano)

The beauty of this dish is that you can use your favorite type of mild white fish and spice it up with the tomato sauce. Good candidates are tilapia, swordfish, bass, halibut, ono, catfish, orange roughy, or flounder. Serve with some warm tortillas and lemon wedges on the side, if you wish.

MAKES 4 ENTREE SERVINGS

SAUCE

1 tablespoon vegetable oil

1 medium onion, chopped

One 14-ounce can diced tomatoes, including the juice

3 or 4 jalapeño peppers, finely chopped

½ cup chopped fresh cilantro

COATING

¼ cup flour

2 tablespoons grated Parmesan cheese

½ teaspoon salt

⅛ teaspoon freshly ground white pepper

Four 6-ounce fish fillets

3 tablespoons vegetable oil

To make the sauce: In a medium skillet, heat the 1 tablespoon vegetable oil over medium heat. Add the onion and cook until tender, about 5 minutes. Add the tomatoes with their juices and the jalapeños, and bring to a boil. Reduce the heat and simmer until the tomatoes are soft, 3 to 4 minutes. Turn off the heat, add the cilantro, and toss lightly. Cover and leave on the stove to stay warm.

To make the coating: Combine the flour, cheese, salt, and white pepper on a plate. Coat the fish fillets until both sides are covered.

In a large skillet, heat the 3 tablespoons oil over medium-high heat. Add the fish fillets in one layer and cook until a light golden brown, 3 to 5 minutes on each side. (The time you cook the fillets will depend on how thick they are.)

Put one fillet on each plate and spoon over the tomato sauce, dividing it evenly. Serve immediately.

VARIATION: *For those with more delicate palates, substitute a 5.75-ounce can of sliced green olives (drained) for the jalapeños.*

⤳ GRILLED SALMON ⤳
WITH CREAMY CILANTRO SAUCE
(Salmon en Salsa Cremosa de Cilantro)

The sauce can be prepared a day ahead if you're making this for a barbecue or dinner party. Although this recipe calls for salmon, feel free to substitute another meaty fish you like, or go crazy and make it with some grilled chicken. Serve with a side of Jicama Salad (page 52), Mexican Rice (page 83), or whatever side dish you like.

MAKES 4 ENTREE SERVINGS

SAUCE
½ cup chopped fresh cilantro
¼ cup Mexican crema
1 tablespoon freshly squeezed lime juice
1 garlic clove, minced
¼ teaspoon ground cumin

   Olive oil
Four 6- to 8-ounce salmon fillets
   Salt

Preheat a grill to high.

To make the sauce: In a small bowl, combine the cilantro, crema, lime juice, garlic, and cumin. Set aside.

Brush a bit of olive oil on both sides of the salmon fillets, season them with salt, and place them on the preheated grill. Grill until the outsides have turned an opaque pink, about 2 minutes on each side.

Place the salmon on 4 separate plates and spoon over the sauce before serving.

ᵜ TILAPIA ᵜ
WITH CHIPOTLE SAUCE
(Tilapia con Salsa Chipotle)

The mildness of the tilapia is a perfect backdrop for the complex flavors and smokiness of the chipotle sauce. Any leftovers make a lovely taco filling the next day. Serve with your choice of salads or sides, accompanied by some warm tortillas.

MAKES 4 ENTREE SERVINGS

1   cup chopped fresh cilantro
4   canned chipotle peppers in adobo sauce, including the sauce
2   tablespoons olive oil
1   tablespoon freshly squeezed lime juice
½   teaspoon ground cumin
½   teaspoon salt
¼   teaspoon freshly ground black pepper
Four 6-ounce tilapia fillets

Preheat a broiler on high.

Combine the cilantro, chipotles, olive oil, lime juice, cumin, salt, and black pepper in a blender or food processor and process until puréed.

Broil the fish until opaque and lightly browned, 3 to 4 minutes on each side.

Place the fillets on 4 separate dishes and spoon over the chipotle sauce. Serve immediately.

⇒ FISH TACOS ⇐

(Tacos de Pescados)

Tacos filled with fresh fish are eaten all along the Baja coast. In San Felipe, a small seaside town in Baja, California, every restaurant along the *malecon* (the waterfront and the center of town) serves this type of fish, battered and fried. And you'd be silly not to try some if you're there. But you don't have to go all the way down to the Gulf of California to enjoy a taste of the ocean. I've created a recipe for you so that you can enjoy your own bit of deliciousness—Baja style. Cervezas and limes are optional.

MAKES 5 ENTREE SERVINGS

- 1 pound firm, white fish (cod, halibut, mahi-mahi, etc.)
- ¾ cup flour
- ½ cup light-colored beer, at room temperature
- 1 egg, separated
- ½ teaspoon dried oregano
- ½ teaspoon freshly ground black pepper
- ¼ teaspoon chili powder
- 1 cup vegetable oil
- Ten 5- to 6-inch Corn Tortillas (page 43 or store-bought)
- 1 cup Mexican crema
- 2 cups shredded cabbage
- Salsa of your choice (optional)
- 10 lime wedges for serving

Cut the fish into 10 strips, 2 to 3 inches long. Dust the fish with ¼ cup of the flour until completely coated.

In a medium bowl, combine the beer, egg yolk, oregano, black pepper, chili powder, and the remaining ½ cup flour until well mixed.

In a separate small bowl, whisk the egg white until small peaks form. Gently fold it into the batter.

In a large saucepan or skillet with high sides, heat about 1 inch of vegetable oil to 350°F. Dredge the fish pieces in the batter, then fry them until golden on both sides, 6 to 8 minutes total, turning to make sure they brown evenly. Remove from the oil to drain on a paper towel–lined plate. Repeat until all the fish is cooked.

Stack the tortillas on a small microwave-safe plate and cover with a wet paper towel. Microwave on high for 30 to 60 seconds, until soft.

Put 2 tortillas on each of 5 plates. Place a piece of fish in each tortilla and top each with a spoonful of crema, a handful of shredded cabbage, and salsa, if you wish. Serve immediately with a couple of lime wedges.

❧ CRAB ENCHILADAS ❧
WITH GREEN MOLE
(Enchiladas de Cangrejo con Mole Verde)

Now that lump crabmeat is more readily available, a great way to enjoy it is with the aromatic spiciness of green mole. This is a rich dish and will go well with a side salad. Of course, you can also use any other kind of enchilada sauce that you like.

MAKES 6 ENTREE SERVINGS

- 2 tablespoons olive or vegetable oil
- 1 red onion, chopped
- 2 stalks celery, chopped
- 1 pound lump crabmeat
- 2 teaspoons chopped fresh oregano
- ½ teaspoon freshly ground black pepper
- 3 cups jarred or fresh Herbed Pumpkin Seed Mole (page 41)
- Twelve 5- to 6-inch Corn Tortillas (page 43 or store-bought)
- 1 cup crumbled cotija cheese
- 3 green onions, chopped
- 1 ripe avocado, pitted (see page 57) and sliced

Preheat the oven to 375°F.

Heat the oil in a large skillet over high heat. Add the onion and celery and cook until slightly limp, about 2 minutes. Add the crab, oregano, and black pepper and toss until the crabmeat is heated through, just another couple of minutes. Remove from the heat.

Spread ½ cup mole verde onto the bottom of a 9-by-13-by-2-inch baking dish.

Stack the tortillas on a microwave-safe plate and cover with a wet paper towel. Microwave on high for 30 to 60 seconds, until softened. Spread the tortillas out onto a couple of large baking sheets or cutting boards.

Spoon some of the crab mixture in a line down the center of each tortilla. Roll them up, placing them seam-side down on the mole verde in the baking dish. Repeat until all of the tortillas are placed in the dish. Pour the remaining mole sauce over the enchiladas and sprinkle with the cheese. Top with the green onions.

Bake until heated through and the cheese melts, about 15 minutes. To serve, transfer 2 enchiladas each onto 6 plates and top with a couple of avocado slices.

GRILLED
❧ SHRIMP BURRITOS ❧
(Burritos de Camarónes al Carbon)

There's something incredibly satisfying about biting into a large flour tortilla stuffed with the smoky goodness of pink shrimp grilled over an open fire. For smaller shrimp, using a grill basket makes cooking them so much easier. For larger shrimp, you can just skewer several at a time and cook them over the flames.

MAKES 4 ENTREE SERVINGS

- 1 pound medium or large shrimp, peeled, deveined, tails removed
- 2 tablespoons freshly squeezed lime juice
- 1 teaspoon ground cumin
- ½ teaspoon chili powder
- ½ teaspoon salt
- 4 large (burrito-size) flour tortillas, warmed
- 2 cups shredded queso fresco
- 2 cups cooked long-grain white or Mexican Rice (page 83)
- 2 cups shredded green or red leaf lettuce
- 1 cup salsa of your choice, plus more for serving
- 4 tablespoons Mexican crema

Preheat a grill to medium heat.

In a medium bowl, combine the shrimp, lime juice, cumin, chili powder, and salt and toss. Cook the shrimp in a grill basket or on large skewers until they turn opaque and pink, 2 to 3 minutes on each side.

Lay the tortillas on separate plates or a large platter. Place ½ cup cheese on each tortilla. Divide the cooked shrimp among the tortillas, placing them in the middle of the tortilla in a line. Top with ½ cup rice and ½ cup lettuce. Spread on ¼ cup salsa and 1 tablespoon crema.

Fold the bottoms and tops of the tortillas over the filling, then roll up as tightly as you can, putting them seam-side down on the plates. Serve immediately with more salsa on the side.

8

DESSERTS AND SNACKS

(Postres y Botanas)

Mexico is naturally blessed with some of the best ingredients for sweets and desserts.

Sugarcane is grown by individual farmers and large plantations. So plentiful is this plant that the canes themselves are sold in bundles and small children chew on their sweet stalks while riding in the backs of open pickup trucks.

Vanilla originated here, and still grows wild into large verdant vines along the edges of the country's tropical rainforests.

Let's not forget the great cacao, the giant pods used to make chocolate. It was so revered, in fact, that the Aztec and Maya considered the processed chocolate to be the drink of the gods. The traditional addition of ground chile to this beautiful cacao makes Mexican chocolate a culinary wonder.

In addition to the ingredients that grow naturally in this tropical paradise, one of the few good things that resulted from the Spanish invasion of the "new" world is cinnamon. Now, we can't imagine Mexican cuisine without this fragrant bark, especially added to Mexican chocolate, ground into mole, and used to coat deliciously warm churros.

I remember the first time I had a churro—the Mexican version of a doughnut. It was from a *panaderia* (bakery) up the street from my family's market. The owner would come out from the back, offering fresh sticks straight out of the fryer, his fingers still coated in cinnamon and sugar as he handed us those striped delights wrapped in crisp waxed paper. His enormous belly would jiggle with his hearty laugh, as flour fell from his large white undershirt, like light snow falling on the checkered floor.

When I was in college, I'd move a couple of times a year, each time making sure that my new apartment was within walking distance of a panaderia. Not only could I enjoy the aromas of freshly baked *pan dulce* (sweet breads), but being near one, I always felt I was part of a community. I could walk in and see old men playing checkers and young mothers clucking at their children, like mother hens gathering their chicks.

Even now, as my house fills with the sweet aromas of Three Milks Cake (page 144) emanating from the oven, I think of the man who would give me the best little pig-shaped cookies in the world. When I lick the cinnamon-sugar from my fingers as the last of the churros has been rolled, I always remember the days of working at my parents' store and how the generosity of a Mexican baker filled me with hope for the rest of my life.

❧ RICE PUDDING ❧
(Arroz con Leche)

Mexicans have long figured out what to do with their leftovers. In this case, this is what they do with leftover white rice. The recipe I've provided is for uncooked rice, but you can use leftover rice by skipping the first ten minutes of cooking. Just add the cinnamon sticks to your rice and milks with the vanilla.

MAKES 6 TO 8 SERVINGS

1   cup uncooked long-grain white rice
2   cinnamon sticks
One 14-ounce can condensed milk
One 14-ounce can evaporated milk
1   cup whole milk
1   teaspoon vanilla extract
    Ground cinnamon for sprinkling

Put the rice and cinnamon sticks into a medium saucepan with 1½ cups of water. Cover and bring to a boil over medium-high heat. Remove the cover and cook until most of the water is evaporated, about 10 minutes. Add the condensed, evaporated, and whole milks and the vanilla and stir. Lower the heat to medium and cook uncovered, stirring, until the rice is tender and the milks thicken, about 15 minutes more. Discard the cinnamon sticks. Remove from the heat and let the rice cool down a bit. The milk will thicken more as it cools.

Spoon into individual serving dishes and sprinkle some ground cinnamon over each serving.

Serve warm or refrigerate to chill, if you like it cold.

VARIATIONS: *You can spice it up by pouring a bit of rum over each dish before serving. If you like yours with a bit of extra texture, stir in ½ cup of raisins after you've discarded the cinnamon sticks and/or sprinkle some sliced almonds on top before you add the ground cinnamon.*

MANGO
PUDDING
(Dulce de Mango)

A tropical end to any meal, this pudding is a great way to enjoy mangoes when they are in season. Look for ripe mangoes that are red and yellow on the outside and have a wonderful fragrance. I always get funny looks at the market when I smell the mangoes, but I'd rather suffer an odd look from a stranger than get an unripe mango.

MAKES 4 OR 5 SERVINGS

3 ripe mangoes

One 14-ounce can evaporated milk

2 tablespoons sugar, plus extra as needed (if your mangoes aren't as ripe and sweet as you thought)

1 tablespoon rum (optional)

Sprigs fresh mint for garnish (optional)

Peel, seed, and cube the mangoes. In a blender or food processor, purée them until smooth. Add the evaporated milk, 2 tablespoons sugar, and rum (if using) and pulse-blend until combined. Taste and add more sugar, if needed. Pour into serving dishes and refrigerate to chill before serving.

When ready to serve, garnish with mint sprigs, if you'd like.

❧ MANGOES ❧
WITH CHILE AND LIME
(Mangoes con Chile y Limón)

Even the tiniest, dustiest streets in Mexico will have a local vendor with a cart piled high with fresh fruits. The señor will cut the fruit for you fresh, douse it with lime juice, and sprinkle some salt and plenty of pure ground chile to make your mouth pucker and water. I love how the sweet fragrance of the mango plays on your tongue with the spice and sour lime.

MAKES 4 SERVINGS
(unless you're a mango hog like me!)

1   dried pasilla or ancho chile, seeded and
    stemmed (see Note)

2   ripe mangoes

1 or 2 lime(s)

    Salt

In a spice grinder or coffee mill, process the dried chile until it becomes a medium-fine powder.

Peel and seed the mangoes and cut them into strips or cubes. Arrange in four separate bowls or on plates.

Grate a bit of lime zest over the mangoes. Then, quarter a lime and squeeze the juice over the mangoes. Sprinkle with a little bit of salt and the powdered chile.

If you want, cut the second lime into slices or wedges and serve on the side for garnish and extra squeezing.

NOTE: *You can buy pure ground chile or premade lime and powdered chile mixes (don't confuse it with chili powder, though, which often has cumin, onion, and garlic powder and other spices mixed in), but I prefer the flavor and aroma of the freshly ground* puro *chile.*

VARIATIONS: *Although I'm providing this recipe with mangoes, you can really make* fruta picada *with any combination of seasonal fruits. Papaya, watermelon, honeydew, cantaloupe, pineapple, apple, orange, and fresh coconut make good options. You can also do the same thing with strips of peeled cucumbers and jícama.*

PLANTAINS
WITH VANILLA AND CINNAMON CREAM
(*Plátanos con Crema de Vainilla y Canela*)

On Mexico's streets, you can see vendors frying up these yellow goodies and topping them with sweetened condensed milk. This is my version, dressed up with real whipped cream, vanilla, and cinnamon. Look for plantains that are so ripe they are nearly or all black. They'll be softer to the touch and sweeter on the tongue.

MAKES 6 SERVINGS
(but fewer people are known to have eaten it all)

¼ cup (½ stick) unsalted butter

3 large, ripe plantains

2 tablespoons granulated sugar

1 cup heavy whipping cream

¼ cup powdered sugar

1 teaspoon vanilla extract

1 teaspoon ground cinnamon

In a large skillet, melt the butter over medium-low heat.

While the butter is melting, peel and slice the plantains into long diagonals, about ½ inch thick. Place the plantains in the butter and cook on both sides over medium heat until golden brown, 4 to 5 minutes on each side. Remove from the heat and sprinkle with the granulated sugar. Cover to keep warm.

In a large bowl, whisk together the cream, powdered sugar, vanilla, and cinnamon until soft peaks form.

Divide the plantains evenly onto 6 dessert plates or bowls, top each with a dollop of the whipped cream, and serve immediately.

SWEET CORN
⮞ ICE CREAM ⮜
(Nieve de Elote)

As would stand to reason, Mexicans love their corn. The grain is a staple in their diet, found in everything from tortillas to tamales to salsas. So, it's no surprise that sweet corn can be found even in ice cream. Using the freshest corn, right from a late-summer harvest, will give you the best results, but any corn will do in a pinch.

MAKES 4 SERVINGS

2   fresh ears of corn, husked
1½ cups whole milk
1   cup heavy whipping cream
½   cup sugar
4   egg yolks
½   teaspoon vanilla extract

Using a grater with large holes, grate the corn kernels and their juices into a large bowl. Discard the cobs.

In a medium saucepan, combine the corn, milk, and cream and bring to a simmer over medium heat.

While the milk mixture is heating up, whisk together the sugar and egg yolks in a bowl until the color is pale yellow and the mixture is thick (just a few minutes).

When the milk mixture begins to simmer, slowly stream in the egg mixture, whisking as you pour. Reduce the heat to low and let simmer, stirring occasionally, until the mixture thickens, about 5 minutes. Remove from the heat and whisk in the vanilla.

Pour the mixture into a bowl and set it in a larger bowl of ice water to cool completely.

Freeze in an ice-cream maker, following the manufacturer's instructions. If you're not serving immediately, transfer to an airtight container and store in the freezer overnight.

WEDGING COOKIES

WEDDING COOKIES

(Biscochos)

If you've never been to a Mexican wedding, you're missing out on some of the best celebrations in the world. Traditionally, these cookies were made for these elaborate celebrations, but now they are popular for holiday baking. The cookies themselves have a long history in Europe and were introduced to Mexico by the Spanish during the seventeenth century. Hence, they are very similar to Russian tea cakes and Spanish *polvorones*.

MAKES 2 DOZEN COOKIES

- 1 cup (2 sticks) unsalted butter, at room temperature
- ¼ cup powdered sugar, plus extra for coating cookies
- 1 teaspoon vanilla extract
- 1 cup all-purpose flour, sifted, plus extra for dusting
- 1 cup pecans, finely chopped

Preheat the oven to 375°F.

In a medium bowl, beat the butter until fluffy. Add the ¼ cup powdered sugar and the vanilla and beat until combined, another couple of minutes. Gradually beat in the 1 cup flour until combined. Then, stir in the nuts.

Dust your hands with flour, then shape the dough into balls using about 1 teaspoon dough for each ball. Place the dough balls about 1 inch apart on an ungreased baking sheet. Bake until lightly golden, 15 minutes.

Transfer the cookies to a rack until they are cool enough to handle but still warm. Roll them in powdered sugar until completely covered.

Serve immediately, or store in a tightly sealed container in the refrigerator or freezer for a couple of weeks.

⇜ CHURROS ⇝

You'll need a cake-decorating tube or piping bag with a large star tip to make the churros into their classic shape. The key to perfect churros (with chewy middles and crispy outsides) is to wait until your oil is hot enough. Otherwise, you'll have soggy, limp churros; and who wants that? Dress up the sweet treats with a side of chocolate dipping sauce or some Mexican Hot Chocolate (page 156).

MAKES ABOUT 24 CHURROS

Vegetable oil
⅓ cup unsalted butter
2 tablespoons brown sugar
½ teaspoon salt
1 cup all-purpose flour
2 large eggs
1 teaspoon vanilla extract
¼ cup granulated sugar
1 teaspoon ground cinnamon

Over medium-high heat, heat a deep skillet with about 2 inches of vegetable oil to 375°F.

While the oil is heating up, add 1 cup of water, the butter, brown sugar, and salt to a large saucepan and bring to a boil. Remove from the heat and quickly stir in the flour until the mixture forms into a ball (it'll take about 1 minute).

In a separate bowl, whisk together the eggs and vanilla, then add to the flour mixture, stirring until well combined. The dough should be sticky.

Combine the granulated sugar and cinnamon on a plate.

Put the dough into a decorating tube or pastry bag fitted with a large star tip. Check that the oil is ready (see note, page 143), then squeeze the dough into the oil, starting from the outside of the pan and spiraling in.

Continued

CHURROS *continued*

Fry until golden brown all over, about 2 minutes on each side. Using a slotted spoon or long wooden chopsticks, remove the churros from the oil and place on a large plate lined with paper towels to absorb the grease. While the churros are still warm, roll them over the cinnamon-sugar mixture until well coated. Repeat until all the dough is used. Cut the churros into 4-inch-long pieces, being careful not to burn yourself.

Enjoy them immediately.

NOTE: *To test your oil without a kitchen thermometer, place a dollop of the dough into the oil. When the oil is hot enough, the dough will begin to bubble up right away.*

THREE MILKS CAKE

(Pastel de las Tres Leches)

A wonderful way to finish off your meal, this traditional favorite is known for its moist richness. It is named "three milks" because of the three different kinds of milk used to soak the cake. Although the cake most likely originated in Mexico, it's popular throughout Latin America.

MAKES 24 SERVINGS

1½ cups cake flour

1   teaspoon baking powder

½   teaspoon salt

½   cup (1 stick) unsalted butter, at room temperature

1   cup granulated sugar

2   teaspoons vanilla extract

5   large eggs

1½ cups whole milk

1¾ cups heavy whipping cream

One 14-ounce can sweetened condensed milk

1   tablespoon powdered sugar

    Ground cinnamon for sprinkling

    Fresh berries for garnish (optional)

Preheat the oven to 325°F. Grease and flour a 9-by-13-inch pan.

In a bowl, sift together the flour, baking powder, and salt and set aside. In a separate bowl, beat together the butter, granulated sugar, and 1 teaspoon of the vanilla until light in color. Add the eggs one at a time, mixing until well combined. Mix in ½ cup of the whole milk, then gently fold in the flour mixture a little bit at a time.

Pour the batter into the pan and bake until it feels firm and a toothpick inserted in the center comes out clean, 30 to 40 minutes.

Let the cake cool to room temperature in the pan. Pierce the cake with a fork several times.

Combine the remaining 1 cup whole milk, 1 cup of the cream, and the condensed milk. Slowly pour over the cooled cake. Refrigerate for 1 hour.

In a mixing bowl, whisk the remaining ¾ cup cream, 1 teaspoon vanilla, and the powdered sugar until medium peaks form. Spread it in a thin layer over the chilled cake. Top with a sprinkle of cinnamon.

Serve garnished with fresh berries, if you wish.

VARIATION: *If you want a "drunken" version* (pastel boracho), *add a bit of rum to the soaking milks before you pour the liquid over the cooled cake.*

CHILE-SPICED PEANUTS

(Cacahuetes en Chile)

Working at my parents' Mexican market, I had the opportunity to try every manner of cookies, candies, and snacks. Although I love the sweet milk *dulces*, one of my all-time favorite snacks is spicy peanuts. The salty, tangy, spicy combination was a joy to eat and just the thought of them makes my mouth water. These chile peanuts can be found in bars all over Mexico, where smart owners keep them out to keep their customers reaching for their beer and margaritas.

MAKES 4 CUPS

- 1 tablespoon olive oil
- 4 cups (1 pound) shelled unsalted, roasted peanuts
- 2 rounded tablespoons chili powder or pure ground chipotle
- 2 teaspoons salt
- 2 tablespoons freshly squeezed lime juice

In a large skillet, heat the oil over medium heat. Add the peanuts and toss occasionally until lightly toasted, 3 to 4 minutes. Turn off the heat (the peanuts will continue to cook in the hot pan). Add the chili powder and salt and toss until the peanuts are well coated.

Squeeze in the lime juice and toss just before serving.

NOTE: *Let the peanuts cool completely and store in an airtight container in the refrigerator for up to a couple of weeks.*

9

BEVERAGES
(Bebidas)

In a land where brightly colored fruits hang heavy from the trees, it's no wonder the culture encourages a bunch of small meals throughout the day. You can eat all you want, whenever you pass a cart tempting you with freshly sliced chunks of coconut, mangoes, melons, and papaya, generously coated with fresh lime juice and a secret concoction of chile powders.

These same fresh fruits are mixed together with a bit of sugar and milk to create gorgeous *paletas*—ice cream bars made with real bits of fruit that surprise you with each frozen bite. These fruits and nuts are turned into fresh *nieves*, too—creamy ice creams that help alleviate the heat of the tropical summers.

And again, the fruits are made into aguas fresca, the refreshing beverages that brighten any meal. There's something wonderfully inviting about a row of chilled jars filled with colorful agua fresca liquids. I smile when I see these large glass *jarritos* filled with creamy white horchata, dark brown tamarindo, and deep red jamaica. The rainbow of colors, ranging from girly pink guava and deeper pink watermelon to light orange cantaloupe and the deep yellow of mango, makes me love summertime even more.

Agua fresca translates to "fresh water" and originated in Mexico. The beverages are made from ripe fruits, rice, seeds, or flower petals blended with sugar and water. The fruits that grow naturally in Latin America are great for making aguas frescas, but any ripe fruit will do. Although my adopted *tías* (aunts) laugh at me when I do it, I've made refreshing drinks from plenty of non-traditional fruits, like blueberries, raspberries, and lychees. So, feel free to take the basic recipes and experiment with your favorite flavors.

The same goes with that quintessentially Mexican drink— the margarita. We've all had bad beverages blended from store-bought margarita mix, but there's no reason to ever do that again when limes are so easily available, ready to be freshly squeezed into your glass, to accompany your carne asadas or fajitas.

When the weather begins cooling down, there are also plenty of hot drinks that warm our stomachs and our hearts.

We especially owe the Central Americans for their discovery of cacao beans. And the word "chocolate" came from the Maya word *xocoatl* and the Aztec *cacahuatl*. This "food of the gods" was consumed for centuries only as a beverage—ground cacao beans mixed with water, wine, and chile peppers—until the Spaniards brought it back to Europe and mixed it with sugar. It was the English who came up with adding milk so that we have our present-day chocolate bars and hot chocolate. I've included a hot chocolate recipe (page 156) with just a bit of spice to warm you up even more.

There are plenty of drink recipes in the following pages to help you quench your thirst, whatever the weather. Try the drinks as they are, or feel free to experiment, adding your own special touches. Perfect for your next backyard barbecue or holiday party, everyone will enjoy the flavors from the land of Kahlúa and Montezuma.

❧ MANGO REFRESHER ❧

(Agua Fresca de Mango)

A refreshing drink for the summer, this tasty beverage is worthy of a celebration. Use fragrant, ripe mangoes to get the best results.

MAKES 2 SERVINGS

1 ripe mango, peeled, pitted, and cut into pieces
1 tablespoon freshly squeezed lime juice
1 tablespoon sugar
   Mint sprigs for garnish (optional)

Combine 1½ cups of water with the mango, lime juice, and sugar in a blender and process until smooth.

Pour into 2 glasses filled with ice and garnish with sprigs of mint, just for fun.

☙ TAMARIND PUNCH ❧
(Agua Fresca de Tamarindo)

One of my favorite flavors, tamarind grows in a brown seed pod that produces a sticky, sweet, tangy pulp that can't be replicated by anything else in the world. Used to make candy and sweets, tamarindo makes a delicious agua fresca, as well. Tamarind pods can be found in the produce section of Mexican, Thai, and Indian markets, as well as some health-food stores.

MAKES 4 SERVINGS

8 ounces (7 to 8 large) tamarind pods
½ cup sugar

Bring 1 quart of water to a boil in a large pot. While the water is boiling, peel off the brittle outer shells of the tamarind pods and put the pods into the boiling water. Add the sugar and stir until it is completely dissolved.

Remove from the heat and let stand for about an hour. Using the back of a wooden spoon, break up the pods to free the pulp from the seeds and then keep mashing until the fibrous material is free from all the pulp.

Pour the mixture through a fine-mesh sieve into a large pitcher, squeezing out as much of the liquid from the fibers and pods as possible.

Refrigerate to chill, if you have the time, or pour over tall glasses filled with ice and serve immediately.

NOTE: *If you're not drinking this immediately, keep covered for up to 5 days in the refrigerator.*

❧ HIBISCUS PUNCH ❧

(Agua Fresca de Jamaica)

The dried petals of the hibiscus flower add a tangy flavor and wonderful color to this festive agua fresca. Double or triple the recipe for your next backyard barbecue, or make a batch as a refreshing summertime drink just for yourself.

MAKES 6 TO 12 SERVINGS

1½ cups sugar
1½ cups jamaica (dried hibiscus flowers)
2 tablespoons freshly squeezed lime juice
    Fresh mint sprigs for garnish (optional)

In a large pot over high heat, bring 3 quarts of water and the sugar to a boil. Remove from the heat and add the jamaica. Let steep for about 15 minutes.

Strain through a fine-mesh sieve into a large, nonreactive bowl or pitcher. Add the lime juice and let cool. Refrigerate until ready to drink. Serve over ice garnished with sprigs of mint, if you like.

NOTE: *Jamaica will stain any plasticware, so be sure to use glass or stainless steel.*

VARIATIONS: *If you want to try some flavor variations, you can add a stick of cinnamon, a handful of whole cloves, or even a few slices of fresh ginger to the pot when you add the flower petals.*

➤ CINNAMON-RICE DRINK ➤

(Agua Fresca de Horchata)

Although horchata has its origins in Spanish cuisines, Mexicans have made it their own, with as many variations as there are regions in Mexico. Traditionally, this *bebida* is made by soaking ground rice overnight, then adding sugar and cinnamon. A wonderful beverage to accompany any meal, it's especially useful to put out that fire in your mouth after taking a bite of a spicy jalapeño. I've tried a number of instant mixes, finding them all gritty and unsatisfactory. So, I devised an easy way to whip up a batch at home, without having to remember to soak the rice overnight. Use Mexican cinnamon and vanilla for the best flavor.

MAKES 4 SERVINGS

6   cups rice milk

½   cup sugar

1½ teaspoons ground cinnamon

1   vanilla bean

4   cinnamon sticks for garnish (optional)

Put the rice milk, sugar, and ground cinnamon into a blender. Cut the vanilla bean in half, lengthwise, and scrape the seeds into the mix. Reserve the pod to make vanilla sugar, Mexican Hot Chocolate (page 156), or for another use. Blend until the sugar is dissolved.

Pour into tall glasses filled with ice and garnish with cinnamon sticks for stirring, if you like.

➤ HOT CORN DRINK ➤

(Atole)

A traditional breakfast drink, atole is a warm, almost porridge-like beverage made with masa. Making a hot drink is a great excuse to break out the traditional wooden whisk, or *molinillo*. The chocolate version is called *champurrado*, but there are myriad variations. Both chocolate and regular versions are popular during Dia de los Muertos (Day of the Dead) and Christmas celebrations. A small town in Michoacán even holds an Atole Festival in March every year, complete with a crowned queen and everything. The drink can be served hot or at room temperature with or without fruits, seeds, and nuts.

MAKES 4 OR 5 SERVINGS

½ cup masa harina

1 vanilla bean, split lengthwise

4 tablespoons chopped piloncillo or packed dark brown sugar

1 cinnamon stick

Combine 5 cups of water and the masa in a blender and blend until smooth. Transfer to a medium saucepan, and scrape in the seeds from the vanilla bean. Then add the vanilla bean husk, piloncillo, and cinnamon stick. Turn up the heat and bring to a boil, stirring frequently until the sugar dissolves.

Remove from the heat and discard the cinnamon stick and vanilla bean husk. At this point you can whisk it, if you like it frothy. Pour into separate mugs and serve hot or warm.

VARIATIONS: *For a fruity beverage, purée some fresh strawberries, pineapple, or banana and add to the mixture after removing the cinnamon and vanilla.*

⤳ HOT CHOCOLATE ⤳

(Chocolate Caliente)

In the central and southern parts of Mexico, people drank chocolate twice a day. Mexicans believed the spirit of the drink was in the foam. A *molinillo* (stirrer or whisk) carved out of wood was used to froth up hot chocolate and Hot Corn Drink (page 155).

MAKES 4 SERVINGS

6 cups milk

½ cup sugar

1 vanilla bean husk (see Note)

1 small dried red chile or
1 teaspoon ancho chile powder

1 teaspoon ground cinnamon

4 ounces unsweetened Mexican chocolate, chopped

4 cinnamon sticks for garnish (optional)

Combine the milk, sugar, vanilla bean husk, chile, and ground cinnamon in a saucepan over high heat and bring to a boil, stirring occasionally. While the liquid is boiling, put the chocolate in a large heat-proof bowl. Once the milk mixture begins to boil, remove from the heat and let it sit for about 5 minutes, to let the vanilla and chile flavors steep a bit. Remove the bean husk and dried chile and discard.

Pour the milk mixture over the chocolate and whisk until the chocolate is completely melted and the drink is frothy.

Divide the hot chocolate among 4 mugs and put a cinnamon stick in each cup, if desired.

NOTE: *The vanilla bean husk is the outside of the vanilla bean after you've scraped out the vanilla seeds inside. It's best to use a nice, supple bean that's not dry and brittle.*

VARIATION: *For a super-rich hot chocolate experience, replace 2 cups of the milk with heavy cream. Then, whip some extra cream with a bit of powdered sugar, spooning a dollop on the top of each cup. Sprinkle with a bit of cinnamon, if you want to be extra fancy.*

❧ MARGARITA ❧
ON THE ROCKS

Although tequila can be had pretty cheaply these days, the agave plant from which the spirit is distilled can take up to a decade to mature. At most Mexican bars, they serve all types of margaritas in glasses rimmed with salt (see note), but some say the salt is a way for bartenders to mask the flavor of cheap tequila. I've provided a recipe for the pure, simple classic, on the rocks. Salt or no salt? You decide.

MAKES 1 SERVING

Ice

2 ounces tequila

¼ cup freshly squeezed lime juice (about 2 limes)

½ ounce triple sec or Cointreau

Coarse-grained salt for rimming (optional)

1 lime wedge for garnish

Fill a cocktail shaker with ice. Add the tequila, lime juice, and triple sec and shake vigorously. Pour into a glass filled with ice, rimmed with salt, if you like. Garnish with a lime wedge.

NOTE: *The easiest way to rim a glass with salt is to spread some salt onto a small plate. After squeezing the lime juice, take the spent lime and rub it over the rim of the glass. Put the glass upside-down into the salt, and the salt will stick to the rim.*

❧ STRAWBERRY MARGARITAS ❧

(Margaritas de Fresa)

For a fruity party drink, nothing beats a blended margarita. Fresh strawberries make a wonderful treat, but feel free to experiment with mangoes, papayas, raspberries, or even blueberries.

MAKES 2 OR 3 SERVINGS

2   cups ice cubes

8 to 10 fresh strawberries, hulled, plus more for garnish

4   ounces tequila

1½ ounces triple sec

1   tablespoon freshly squeezed lime juice

Coarse sugar for rimming

Lime slices for garnish (optional)

Combine the ice, strawberries, tequila, triple sec, and lime juice in a blender and process until all of the ice chunks have been blended.

Pour into glasses rimmed with coarse sugar (see Note, page 158) and garnish with fresh strawberries or lime slices, if you'd like.

VARIATION: *To make a virgin version, omit the tequila and triple sec and add a bit more lime juice.*

⟿ CACTUS FRUIT COCKTAILS ⟿

(Margaritas de Tunas)

Cactus fruits, also known as "prickly pears," are any number of fruit nodules that grow wild on the nopales cactus in the deserts of Mexico and the southwestern United States. Although prickly pear juice is sold in bottles, nothing compares to the sweet taste of their fresh flesh and spitting out the numerous seeds. My dad taught me how to peel the fruits: Hold them with a pair of thick leather or work gloves, cut off both ends, cut a slit down the length of the fruit, then remove the prickly skins with a pair of tongs. Although they come in a variety of flavors and colors, I find the ones with the bright pink flesh to be the most tasty and the drinks from them come out more festive looking, too.

MAKES 2 SERVINGS

4   prickly pears, peeled
    Ice
4   ounces tequila
1½ ounces triple sec
1   tablespoon freshly squeezed lime juice
1   tablespoon sugar
    Coarse-grained salt for rimming (optional)
    Lime slices for garnish (optional)

Place the prickly pears in a blender and pulse until liquefied. Strain the juice into a small bowl (you should have about 1 cup of juice).

Fill a large cocktail shaker with ice, add the prickly pear juice, tequila, triple sec, lime juice, and sugar and shake vigorously.

Pour into glasses filled with ice, rimmed with salt or sugar, if you like (see Note, page 158). Garnish with lime slices.

VARIATION: *For a fancy party cocktail, combine some chipotle chile powder with your coarse-grained salt before rimming the glasses. The smoky, spicy salt will make a nice complement to the sweet, fruity drink.*

QUICK AND EASY
➤ MEXICAN MENUS ➤

Abuelita's Breakfast
Turkey Chilaquiles (page 103)
Hot Corn Drink (page 155)

Light Summer Lunch
Shrimp Cocktail (page 121)
Carne Asada Salad (page 49)
Margarita on the Rocks (page 158)

Barbecue Fiesta
Jícama Salad (page 52)
Seasoned Skirt Steak (page 109)
Mango Salsa (page 34)
Baked Tortilla Chips (page 45)
Mango Refresher (page 150)

Fancy Dinner Party
Chilled Avocado-Lime Soup (page 61)
Veracruz-Style Fish (page 123)
Plantains with Vanilla and Cinnamon Cream (page 138)
Cactus Fruit Cocktails (page 161)

Street Food at Its Best
Chile-Spiced Peanuts (page 147)
Spicy Corn on the Cob (page 81)
Overstuffed Chicken Sandwiches (page 94)

Turn Up the Heat
Smoky Chipotle Salsa (page 32)
Chicken with Mole Sauce (page 97)
Roasted Poblano Chiles (page 76)
Mexican Hot Chocolate (page 156)

Just For the Kids
Beef Flautas (page 107)
Crispy Chicken Taquitos (page 100)
Mexican Wedding Cookies (page 140)
Mango Refresher (page 150)

Vegetarian Delight
Fried Potatoes with Poblano Chiles (page 77)
Fried Chayote Squash (page 79)
Aztec Zucchini (page 78)
Corn Tortillas (page 43)
Mango Pudding (page 135)

Enough to Feed an Army
Beef Enchiladas with Red Sauce (page 108)
Mexican Rice (page 83)
Refried Beans (page 74)
Three Milks Cake (page 144)
Hibiscus Punch (page 153)

MAIL-ORDER SOURCES

These days, it's usually easy to find a Mexican grocery store in your neighborhood or even an aisle of Latino staples in your regular supermarket. Even if you can't, you're in luck because so many ingredients are now available by mail order or via the Internet. You can also look for *carnicerias* (butchers), *panaderias* (bakeries), *fruterias* (fruit sellers), or *tortillerias* (tortilla makers) in your area.

Amazon.com
Not just for books anymore, Amazon sells everything but the kitchen sink. No, wait—they sell kitchen sinks, too! But since we're talking about Mexican ingredients, they have a pretty extensive collection. Most ingredients are sold through third-party sellers, but this is a convenient site to search for specific items you may need.

Gourmet Sleuth
P.O. Box 508
Los Gatos, CA 95031
408-354-8281
www.gourmetsleuth.com
Specializing in a variety of ethnic ingredients, they have a slew of jarred moles, tamarind paste, jamaica, achiote, and even epazote (dried and jarred).

Mesa Mexican Foods
P.O. Box 40663
Mesa, AZ 85274
www.mesamexicanfoods.com
Although they may not have as extensive a catalog as Mexgrocer (below), they do have authentic ingredients you may not be able to find elsewhere, such as raw cacao beans and small packets of Tapatio brand hot sauce. They also sell a tamale-making kit, if you're ready for a bit of culinary adventure.

Mexgrocer
4060 Morena Blvd., Suite C
San Diego, CA 92117
800-463-9476
www.mexgrocer.com
They may not have the lowest prices on items, but this online mercado (market) is an incredibly comprehensive resource for Mexican ingredients. Looking for tamarind soda? They've got it. Mole? Salsas? Masa? Spices? They've got them all. You can even get your favorite saint candle or a golden rosary answer to your prayers.

❧ BOOKS ❧
ON THE FOODS, COOKING, AND CULTURE OF MEXICO

Bayless, Rick. *Authentic Mexican: Regional Cooking from the Heart of Mexico.* New York, NY: William Morrow, 1987, 2007.

———. *Mexican Everyday.* New York, NY: W. W. Norton, 2005.

Butt, John, and Carmen Benjamin. *A New Reference of Modern Spanish.* Hightstown, NJ: McGraw-Hill, 2004.

Castro, Lourdes. *Simply Mexican.* Berkeley, CA: Ten Speed Press, 2009.

Daigneault, Joe [a.k.a. Mad Coyote Joe]. *A Gringo's Guide to Authentic Mexican Cooking.* Flagstaff, AZ: Northland Publishing, 2001.

Feniger, Susan, and Mary Sue Milliken. *Cocina: The Best of Casual Mexican Cooking.* Menlo Park, CA: Sunset Publishing Corp., 1996.

Franz, Carl, and Lorena Havens (authors), Steve Rogers (editor). *The People's Guide to Mexico.* Berkeley, CA: Avalon Travel Publishing, 2006.

Joseph, Gilbert M., and Timothy J. Henderson. *The Mexico Reader: History, Culture, Politics.* Durham, NC: Duke University Press, 2003.

Kennedy, Diane. *The Art of Mexican Cooking.* New York, NY: Clarkson Potter, 1989, 2008.

———. *The Essential Cuisines of Mexico.* New York, NY: Clarkson Potter, 2000, 2009.

Kernecker, Herb. *When in Mexico, Do as the Mexicans Do.* Hightstown, NJ: McGraw-Hill, 2004.

Levick, Melba (photography), and Elizabeth E. McNair (text). *Mexicocina.* San Francisco, CA: Chronicle Books, 2006.

Martinez, Zarela. *The Food and Life of Oaxaca: Traditional Recipes from Mexico's Heart.* Hoboken, NJ: Wiley, 1997.

Meyer, Michael C., William L. Sherman, and Susan M. Sherman. *The Course of Mexican History.* New York, NY: Oxford University Press, 2006.

Righter, Evie. *The Best of Mexico.* New York, NY: William Morrow, 1992.

Rivera, Guadalupe, and Marie-Pierre Colle. *Frida's Fiestas: Recipes and Reminiscences of Life with Frida Kahlo.* New York, NY: Clarkson Potter, 1994.

❧ INDEX ❧

TABLE OF
➤ EQUIVALENTS ➤

The exact equivalents in the following tables have been rounded for convenience.

LIQUID/DRY MEASUREMENTS

U.S.	METRIC
¼ teaspoon	1.25 milliliters
½ teaspoon	2.5 milliliters
1 teaspoon	5 milliliters
1 tablespoon (3 teaspoons)	15 milliliters
1 fluid ounce (2 tablespoons)	30 milliliters
¼ cup	60 milliliters
⅓ cup	80 milliliters
½ cup	120 milliliters
1 cup	240 milliliters
1 pint (2 cups)	480 milliliters
1 quart (4 cups, 32 ounces)	960 milliliters
1 gallon (4 quarts)	3.84 liters
1 ounce (by weight)	28 grams
1 pound	448 grams
2.2 pounds	1 kilogram

LENGTHS

U.S.	METRIC
⅛ inch	3 millimeters
¼ inch	6 millimeters
½ inch	12 millimeters
1 inch	2.5 centimeters

OVEN TEMPERATURES

FAHRENHEIT	CELSIUS	GAS
250	120	½
275	140	1
300	150	2
325	160	3
350	180	4
375	190	5
400	200	6
425	220	7
450	230	8
475	240	9
500	260	10